T0078246

Wrestling with the Goddess

Wrestling with the Goddess

A Personal Odyssey

Azeem Kayum

Wrestling with the Goddess
A Personal Odyssey

iUniverse books may be ordered through booksellers or by contacting:

iUniverse
1663 Liberty Drive
Bloomington, IN 47403
www.iuniverse.com
844-349-9409

ISBN: 978-0-5954-8564-2 (sc)
ISBN: 978-0-5957-1957-0 (hc)

Print information available on the last page.

iUniverse rev. date: 01/22/2022

To all my peers who are challenged.

To my mom Laila, my dad Faizal, my sister Lisaan and those extended family members who believe in me.

To the doctors and nurses who provided the delicate care I needed.

To my teachers, who guided me throughout my school years.

To my friends who accept me the way I am.

My Motto

"Reach for the stars. They may seem far. Persevere and you will get there."

Contents

Foreword

I first met Azeem when I interviewed his mother, Laila, for a special article I was doing on breast cancer. At that time I was faced with a journalistic challenge. I was torn between a desire to continue with my assignment or drop everything and write a story about this young man's life. I took the easy path and wrote about his mother, but something about Azeem touched my heart. I still wanted to tell his story because it's unique, heartwarming and very special—like him.

I didn't have to do this because Azeem has written his own story. He asked me to read the manuscript and make suggestions. How can one make suggestions about words that come from the heart? I did not suggest a change in any word. Azeem's story isn't an easy read, but it's gripping in its brutal honesty and the stark reality that it may never have been written. *Challenge* is a word Azeem is familiar with and by reading his story, one can actually feel the challenges he faced in his young life. His story is not one that makes the reader feel sorry for him; on the contrary, his story is real and everyone can relate to it. It's about trials and tribulations, disappointment and despair, anger and angst, hope and hurt, support and sharing and most of all about the power of love—love of family and friends who helped support Azeem and enabled him to defy so many odds and become a role model and an inspiration for people who take life and living for granted.

Raheel Raza
Media consultant, freelance writer and author

Acknowledgements

Writing about my own life was extremely difficult. It was a real struggle for me to put my thoughts into words. It meant reliving some experiences that caused great pain. People who were aware of my project encouraged me to finish it. There are too many names to mention and I am sure those people know who they are. Their belief in me gave me the strength and confidence to complete this work. I thank all of you.

Preface

There are times in a medical career when it is gratifying to be proven wrong. My first few conversations with the family of Azeem were not easy for them to hear.

Those conversations were sprinkled with discouraging phrases: "severely damaged …," "can't breathe on his own …," "these children do not live very long." And later, when he was two and a half years old, "he is not doing well—he may be 'brain dead.' We'll just have to wait and see." To ensure that he did not suffer further damage, we recommended the insertion of a tracheostomy tube into his trachea. His parents were always against having this surgical procedure performed, but we felt that it was the only way to safely sustain his life.

Now he is an adult. I have attended his graduation, where he received his college diploma with honours in radio broadcasting. So it is a real pleasure to be proven wrong!

Reading this account of Azeem's story is sometimes difficult. He and his family have been severely tested by the challenges thrown at them. He is sometimes angry; who wouldn't be? But by reading this account we may be able to share a small part of the difficulties faced by those who are disabled. We may not be able to walk a mile in his shoes, but we can share a few steps, share his experiences, and share the support and love he has received from his family.

The quiet courage shown by Azeem and his family outweighs the anger and will be the strength that he requires to go on. However, his life will continue to be a challenge, and he will have to face many more obstacles in the years ahead. This account shows that he now has his own opinions, his own aspirations, and the determination to overcome future challenges.

He has already fulfilled one of his first ambitions. He is "an inspiration to others with disabilities," and I believe that he is also an inspiration to the non-disabled segment of society. This account of his life, from his perspective, will enlighten us all and perhaps cause us to be more sensitive to the challenges that the disabled encounter on a daily basis.

Dr. John Edmonds, M.D., B.S., F.R.C.P.C.
The Hospital for Sick Children, Toronto

Introduction

This is my story, told in my own words. My parents were the first readers, and with my approval they made some minor changes. I reminded them since it was my story and not theirs, I needed to tell it from my perspective. I am happy they respected my wishes.

I am brain damaged. The language part of my brain is the most affected. My teachers, psychologists and others who tested me will be shocked to know that I actually wrote about my life. Those in different professions had written me off many times. Some people still look at me and think that I'm stupid. Many ignore me, and yes, there are some who could not care less. On the other hand, there are those who love and care for me. And there are those who make time for me.

It is because of the efforts of all of those wonderful people who continue to stand by me that I am confident enough to put my thoughts together and write about my life. The pages you read will be about experiences and events that affected me. Some were pleasant; others were not. I decided to let it all out, as much as I can remember. My trials and triumphs will hopefully serve as a lesson and an inspiration to others.

This book took me several years to complete because I really had to struggle to think about how to write. No one truly understands my deep feelings. I have kept a lot of it inside until now.

I have had to describe specific experiences to show the depth of pain and hurt I endured as well as the fun and pleasures I enjoyed. At times I experienced anger, resentment, happiness and merriment. Some may be upset and offended with what I

1

have written. My story is not meant to displease anyone. It is my way of letting you know that even though I may not look, walk, talk, sleep and think like others, I am still a human being.

I was born with disabilities and those became more noticeable as I grew older. Nobody expected me to do much in life, but my parents, my sister, special doctors, nurses, teachers, family, and exceptional friends never gave up on me. It is because of them I have accomplished so much. Nothing is automatic and easy for me. I have to be taught everything—from the simplest to the most complex. Today, I continue to have a hard time doing most things, but I get them done.

I must first mention my parents, who have given up a lot for me. From as far back as I can remember, my dad has always been there for me. He used many of his vacation days so he could be with me in the hospital anytime I was admitted, and that was often. He prayed over me every night for many years. Now I am quite capable of saying my own prayers. He still changes my tracheostomy tube (referred to as a trache) and washes my hair.

Yes, we also had some fun. We went bowling, played tennis and he tried to teach me how to play cricket. We attended some wrestling and other sporting events, and a few concerts. We took family vacations in Florida, Maryland and Trinidad and Tobago. If given the opportunity, my dad would continue to take me out, but after all, no young man really wants to be out with his dad all the time. Instead, I would prefer to jump in my own sports car and go out with people my own age. But only some of them find the time for me. Only a few are prepared to be seen in public with me. Sadly, despite all the public awareness programmes about people with disabilities, we are still treated differently, shunned and isolated in so many ways.

My mom was and still is the teacher. She is responsible for my academic success. She, her aunt in Montreal, her cousins, and her sisters followed my progress every step of the way.

It must have been tough on her, because I know it is not easy for me to learn. She gave up her career and the most productive phase of her life so she could cater to my endless needs, from teaching to physiotherapy.

My time on earth has been extended not just once or twice, but on several occasions. Sometimes I feel I do not have much longer. Since that awful night on December 8, 1979, my days have been numbered—a few days, a few weeks, and a few months. I am not out of the woods, as I still depend on life-support systems to help me breathe.

So, why procrastinate in writing about my life? Whatever little time I have left, I want everyone to know about my experiences and perhaps imagine living my life for a day or two. My attitude toward life has made me face things differently. It has made me stronger. I have several disabilities, but the fighter in me allows me to accept them and do everything within my power to be the person I want to be. My parents did not write me off the way some people did. They showed me how I can achieve. They taught me to believe in myself. It is that belief which has also motivated me to write this book. Who would have thought that such a thing was possible? Now it is my turn to help others through this effort. Who knows? Maybe that is why God has been extending my life over and over again, so I could be a living lesson to others.

It is my sincere wish that everyone learns something after reading my story. Hopefully, it will help those who are "normal" to get a better understanding of what a less fortunate person goes through in life. I have endured physical pain from many operations and mental pain from those people who choose to isolate, ignore and treat me differently. By writing about my experiences,

I am reaching out to both the physically and mentally challenged and especially the normal people. Although I do not appear normal in their eyes, I have feelings! I do not want anyone to feel sorry for me. I cannot stand pity. It is the last thing I want. You see, there are times when I forget I am disabled. It is those normal people who remind me that I have disabilities. If some understand my message and change their attitude and behaviour toward the disabled, then I would have achieved another victory.

With the gift of life that God has granted me, I would like to make a difference in this world. I may not be able to change the entire world, but if I can change a few of the people in it, one person at a time, then I would be grateful.

So for now this effort is my way of raising more awareness about the ongoing challenges faced by people with disabilities. Help me make a difference!

Chapter 1

Adding Insult to Injury

"You are a bad outcome from a good delivery." Those words were said to me directly. And they hurt—even today, so many years later.

When I was about fourteen, I turned to the obstetrician who uttered those insulting words and said, "If I am a bad outcome from a good delivery, as you say, why am I the way I am?"

I looked at my parents. From my mom's expression, I knew she was furious. She was boiling with anger. Her teeth were clenched and her nose was flaring. If she had something in her hand, she might have clobbered that insensitive man. Glancing at my dad, I could see he looked calm, but those words affected him also. He was dying to say something. But I prayed he did not utter a word because his words bite—and really hard too, especially when anyone says or does hurtful things.

The sad thing was the doctor never thought he said anything wrong. He simply continued, "The doctor did everything right," looking directly at me.

"If he did, why do I need a respirator to help me breathe at nights? Why am I unable to walk like everyone else? Why is my brain so messed up?" I belted out the questions. "You can't imagine how much I have struggled in my life. Everything I have to do takes so much time. And you're sitting there telling me the doctor did everything right?" The words stormed out of my mouth like a hurricane. Who was he to insult me like that? He was educated and I was a brain-damaged teenager. But that did not give him the right to tell me those hurtful things. I was able to understand what he said. But his insensitivity did not matter to him. He was probably covering up for his fellow doctor.

My parents did not believe what they were hearing. Even I could not believe those questions and statements were coming out of my mouth. Me, a fourteen-year-old, talking to a medical expert the way I was. Surprisingly, my parents did not stop me. My dad always told me I can "disagree without being disagreeable." My tone of voice was angry. My voice has always been rough and coarse, probably because of the number of times tubes have been sent down my airway. Perhaps the obstetrician felt I was a rude teenager. I was blunt. I spoke my mind and I felt the doctor heard me loud and clear. My brain was not normal, but I knew the doctor was not only insulting me, but he was also saying things to make me feel stupid. Little did he know that even at that tender age, I had acquired a lot of self-confidence because of the manner in which my parents brought me up.

Because of the damage I suffered at birth, I could not move or breathe. My parents told me I looked grey. The doctors had to give me oxygen and hook me up to a respirator. They connected me to lots of wires, tubes and monitors. My mom told me I moved and kicked when she was carrying me. So, I think somebody messed up when delivering me and messed me up as a result! I remember reading "high cervical cord injury at birth." Something happened at birth. Was it the doctor's fault? From where I stand—and yes, I can stand and walk—it seems to me the doctor who delivered me did something that should not have been done. But what?

The obstetrician to whom I spoke assured me that "the doctor did everything right." Yet, there was some serious brain damage.

That does not sound "right" to me. How could "everything right" turn out to be so wrong? I'm happy that I still have enough grey matter to write about my experiences. It all has to do with the power of God, the mind, the support of family and friends, and showing others that not everything is carved in stone. Doctors said I would not live. Some teachers did not think I could learn. One psychologist went as far as saying I should not be reading! They were going by the book. I don't blame them for that. I was different.

Often when I sit and think about my condition, I wonder whether the doctor who delivered me ever reflects on my life— on what became of me or what quality of life I enjoy. Perhaps I am just a number to him.

Despite my condition, my parents, some special doctors and nurses at The Hospital for Sick Children in Toronto (also called Sick Kids) worked hard to keep me alive. What a fantastic job they did! My life, however, has been tough and my experiences an eye-opener. My parents, doctors, teachers, family members and friends all have learned: I am a person, a living human being, with blood flowing through my veins. *I have feelings just like you.*

I may not be normal in many people's eyes, but I am living my life to its fullest, despite the limitations. Is it tough? Yes! Isolating? Oh, yes! Hurtful? Many times! Am I better? Not completely. I have taught many people lots of things. I have accomplished a great deal in my challenged life and that, in my mind, is living. I truly believe that making the best out of a bad situation is more meaningful than sitting around feeling sorry for myself.

Chapter 2
Long-Term Care

My brain goes to sleep whenever I do. At times, my breathing becomes very shallow and shuts off completely. And, yes, I can die if I sleep for a few nights without my respirator. When I was two-and-a-half years old, a tracheostomy tube was inserted into my trachea to help with my breathing. It's still there. What an inconvenience the tube is and what a greater obstacle the machine is. What a pain to deal with, and I do not mean physical pain. It's not something a young man would like to have, especially for social reasons. How I wish I could breathe on my own. But then, that same tube and machine are my lifeline.

Many times early in my life the doctors thought I was going to die. In fact, when I was a few days old, the doctors asked my parents to place me in an institution. I often think about what I would have been like today if they had decided to do so. From what I have seen in some institutions, I might not have survived, or if I did, I would still be paralysed and perhaps I would have proven the doctors right by becoming a vegetable. Judging from what I have observed during my visits to institutions, the nurses provide care, but they do not have the time to give anyone too much individual attention. They do the best they can.

My parents said I needed lots of care and stimulation. I am very grateful to them for making so many sacrifices to care for me at home. I know it has been tough for them. As I grow older,

I continue to realize how difficult it must have been. They were still in their twenties, young and career-oriented, but, knowing I would need constant care, they agreed to take me home. It would have been easier for them to put me away and move on with their lives. It was just the two of them, without much extended family to depend on. They did not have any medical training or background. They had just immigrated to Canada, my dad from Guyana and my mom from Trinidad. They worked at entry-level positions. And in those days, there was little or no government funding for home and nursing care.

Even my two primary doctors at The Hospital for Sick Children, Dr. John Edmonds and Dr. Karen Pape, were quite concerned about the decision my parents made to care for me at home. Yet, the hospital could not keep me any longer. I had spent the first year and eleven days in their loving care. They could not do anything more for me. They had tried everything they knew at the time to keep me alive. Despite my survival, they believed it was a matter of weeks or months before I would die. The damage I suffered at delivery was so severe they knew that even though I had defied all the odds during those three hundred and seventy-six days, with many near-death experiences, cardiac arrests, lung collapses, seizures and chest infections, my days were numbered.

I was sent home from Sick Kids with a negative pressure ventilator. That was a monstrous machine, which was described in my mom's book, *For a Breath of Life—The True Story of a Boy's Resilience and His Family's Determination (1995)*, as "an iron lung … the body is enclosed in a clear, hard plastic box … and the head remains outside." I used that machine for many months, and I still cannot understand how I slept in one position all the time. Thank God I don't remember those days.

The purpose of that type of ventilation was to stimulate the breathing. "Once the machine was activated, the body moved.

This movement then triggered the diaphragm to function and enabled the patient to breathe," my mom explained. She wrote the book to give other parents encouragement in their care for children with disabilities. She talked about the struggles both she and my dad faced, especially with the different levels of government, "the bureaucratic nightmare," as she termed it. She stressed how important it is to fight for what you believe in. If she and my dad had accepted what the bureaucrats, the doctors or even the school consultants had said, I would not have accomplished as much.

As I grew older, I read and heard about my early years. I am still amazed about their decision to care for me at home. After all, when I was discharged from The Hospital for Sick Children, my mom was seven months pregnant with my sister, Lisaan.

Were my parents crazy to take me home under those circumstances? Maybe they were, but I am very happy they did. They told me they could not bear the thought of putting me away. While it would have been acceptable, considering how ill I was, they just could not do it and took a huge leap of faith. I am very lucky they did.

Not too many people understand the care I needed and still continue to need. I look well most of the time and people assume I am fine. However, my condition is still fragile and a simple chest infection can lead to complications, even death. When Severe Acute Respiratory Syndrome (SARS) broke out in Toronto in 2003, I was very worried. With my condition, if I develop pneumonia, I could be dead within days. My parents were also quite concerned. My mom had spoken to our family doctor when she went into voluntary quarantine after visiting a local hospital. Fortunately, she never developed the illness. My parents become quite edgy when I get sick with just a regular cold. They do not show how anxious they are, but I can sense the tension. They try to avoid any family or public gatherings, especially when a serious virus is in the air.

No one except God knows how long I will live. I could outlive my parents or I could become very ill and my parents would not be able to care for me. They are getting older and so am I. They could become frail and weak. Then what? Long-term care in an institution? I hope and pray that day never comes!

Chapter 3

Faith

While I am not as God-conscious as my father, I strongly believe the leap of faith, which my parents took when I was a year and eleven days old, worked wonders for me. Their strong faith has guided them: it has given them the courage and strength to stand up for my medical and educational rights; it has given them the confidence and inspiration to face their own personal challenges and adversities; and it has made other families dealing with their problems look at my parents as great role models. They have been using the knowledge they gained from caring for me to counsel other families who have disabled children. They do this without thinking twice, and all voluntarily.

My mom was diagnosed with breast cancer in September 1999. Once the cancer was confirmed, she decided to inform all her family and friends. I remember after she found out the number of hours she spent on the phone one night "telling the world." Of course, since we are Canadians of East Indian and Indo-Caribbean heritage, it was not the normal thing to do. It should have been kept very private. But for my mom, telling others was the beginning of the healing process. She believed she was going to use her energy to get better, not to keep her cancer a secret. My parents have never believed in keeping any illness quiet. They believe that no one asks to get sick, so if someone is diagnosed with a heart condition or any other sickness, there is nothing to be ashamed of. Many people don't like to say they have cancer or another illness, and I find that strange.

Our family also believes strongly in the power of prayer, and I am a living example of that power. I am convinced that I would not have survived if so many people were not praying for me. By making her cancer public, my mom also wanted to tap into the greatest source of healing—prayer. Many of our friends, people from different religious backgrounds, held group prayers. I think all the prayers have helped.

So, once my mom told the family and her friends about the diagnosis, she put her mind to the task of surgery and treatment. Going through that was not easy, especially since all her sisters and close relatives were not around to talk to. She is still suffering from the effects of the cancer, which has left her with a condition known as lymphedema. Unfortunately, she is one of a small percentage of women whose lymphedema is permanent. Yet, her faith continues to guide and motivate her. She has been using her experience and knowledge to help other breast cancer victims cope. She has made a few public appearances, sharing her story and giving others hope.

My mom's diagnosis scared me. I wondered whether she would die. Although cancer can be treated successfully, I could not help feeling worried and insecure. What would happen to me? She has always been there for me. How would I go on? Seeing her go through the treatment was hard. She was sick, tired, and depressed. There was nothing I could do to make her feel better. There were days when she could not do anything. Yet, few people would have known she was that sick. She took great pride in making herself look good. I prayed really hard. I believe God responded by giving my mom the strength to get better and deal with the effects of the illness.

I know my dad's deep-rooted faith has played a major role in my development. While he never imposes his beliefs and values upon my sister and me, we cannot help but admire and try to follow him. We have been told that "example is the best teacher," and my dad is an excellent role model in that respect. He is practical as far as religion is concerned. He observes and respects everyone's religion.

My mom believes in prayer. She has seen how effective it is. Like my dad, she knows that it is important to have religion in her life. My sister and I benefit from their beliefs. We are both reminded on a regular basis about the value of prayer and the importance of being good and caring individuals.

I know that most children regard their parents as role models. I look up to mine a lot because few parents would have done what they did for me. Few parents would have stayed together.

In fact, we know of many families caring for children with disabilities who could not stick it out and ended up being separated and even divorced. Marriage is for better or for worse. In the case of my parents, it often has been for worse; but I think it is because of their strong belief in God that they have remained together. They took a bad situation and made it into something good. It was not easy to deal with my hundreds of needs. It still isn't. My care requires a lot of personal sacrifices and in that regard, on a scale of one to ten; I would give my parents a ten.

The challenges they have had to deal with have brought my parents closer together and make their love for each other stronger. My sister and I see the love and affection they share every day. It is great to see them hug one another and to hear their laughter. They never seem to carry around their burdens. I often hear people comment, "I don't know how you guys do it."

I think it is their deep faith—faith in the Creator, faith in his wisdom, faith in his mercy, faith in knowing he is always there, faith in knowing he will continue to give them the strength to face each challenge with courage and humility. It is that same faith, that precious gift my parents have given to me, that keeps me going.

It is appropriate to end this chapter by quoting my mom's favourite inspirational verse, which is hanging on a wall in our home:

Footprints

One night a man had a dream.
He dreamed he was walking along the beach with the Lord.
Across the sky flashed scenes from his life.
For each scene, he noticed two sets of footprints in the sand.
One belonged to him, and the other to the Lord.
When the last scene of his life flashed before him, he looked back at the footprints in the sand.
He noticed that many times along the path of his life there was only one set of footprints.
He also noticed that it happened at the very lowest and saddest time in his life.
This really bothered him and he questioned the Lord about it.

"Lord, you said that once I decided to follow you, you'd walk with me all the way.
But, I have noticed during the most troublesome times in my life, there is only one set of footprints. I don't under-stand why when I needed you most you would leave me."

The Lord replied, "My precious, precious child, I love you and I would never leave you.
During your times of trial and suffering, when you see only one set of footprints, it was then that I carried you."

That special hand continues to carry my family on a daily basis. There are days when I feel they are burdened. There are days when obstacles are thrown at them, even unnecessary ones. Somehow, they pick themselves up and move on. God gives them that strength. He carries them when they are torn, beaten and battered. The beauty of it all is nobody can tell.

They are truly blessed!

Chapter 4

Learning to Learn

"He will never walk. He will never talk." Those words echoed in the hospital room. Shortly after I was born, my parents sat and listened to the doctors as they gave me a death sentence. My mom told me that the words "came hurling from all around the room. I thought I was going crazy hearing 'paralysed, brain-damaged and institution.'" The doctors even went further to say that if I survived, I would be a "complete vegetable." To their surprise, I survived. And I am very far from being a vegetable. Maybe that's why I am not fond of eating vegetables!

When I was five years old, my IQ was tested and it was too low to be scored. Imagine that! If I had been left as I was, my IQ might have been virtually non-existent today. I had to be taught how to grasp a toy, how to crawl, how to sit on a chair. I could not do any of those things. But my parents worked with me. They took the little I had and fed, nurtured and developed it.

One day I talked to my mom about my struggles as a little boy. We mainly discussed things I do not remember. She told me the story about how she and Dad taught me to sit on a little chair.

"Your father and I bought you a table and chair set so that you could sit on the chair and do your colouring. You did other things like pasting and matching also. After we mounted the furniture, we thought you would be anxious to sit on the chair. Instead, you opted to stand and quickly began colouring. I pulled the chair out so you would have more room. You looked at me and continued with your activity. I then turned the chair toward you and told you to sit. Again, you looked at me and casually continued with the colouring. Your father placed you closer to the chair with the hope you would sit on it. It never happened."

I could not believe what I was hearing. "So what did you do?"

"We realized that you just did not know what to do. You understood what we were asking you to do, but could not figure out the steps."

"Did I try?"

"You made some effort, but it was obvious that the process was tough. Your father and I then began teaching you. We first positioned you near the chair. It was the right height, so you did not have to climb. With your back facing the seat, we applied a little pressure on your shoulder. Your father bent your knees and you sat on the chair."

"Was I able to do it on my own after that?"

"No, we had to practise that for a few days, repeating it two or three times a day. Once you developed the confidence, you were fine."

My mom went on to tell me that she and my dad were heartbroken, but they were not going to quit.

I sometimes wonder why I have to go through so many difficulties. I have the sense to realize how different things could have been and that bugs me. People say everyone goes through hardships in life. I agree. I also know there are others who go through more. I count my blessings, but I wonder if the normal people really understand what it is like to be sick from birth to adulthood.

I get blisters from the tape that holds the tube in place around my neck. I suffer from regular colds and have to struggle to cough and get the mucus out. When I was younger, I had to be suctioned in order to clear my lungs. I have been sleeping with the aid of a respirator every night since I was two-and-a-half years old.

While my challenges are physical, mental, and long-term, I cannot tolerate people feeling sorry for me. I'm not normal and will never be normal, but I have a lot to be grateful for. I'm blessed with a loving and supportive family, some caring extended family, and a few close family friends. What more can I want? Perhaps to be normal!

But then, what is normal? Is it being like some teenagers or young adults, out late at night and getting into trouble? That may seem normal to some. Is it studying all evening and night with no social life? Is it staring at someone who dresses and looks differently and laughing? That may be normal to many.

Despite all my shortcomings and my medical condition, I am a happy person. Sure, I have bad days, but during those periods I always try to think about the good things in my life. I remember going on day trips to Niagara Falls, CN Tower, Centre Island, Ottawa and other places of interest. When I was younger I recall my mom educating me on the height and size of the falls. She talked about how falls really came about. I was fascinated with the history of that place of wonder. I had the fright of my life when I followed my sister and went in the Horror House on Main Street, Niagara. I learned the hard way not to follow others.

We had a blast at Centre Island. We took the ferry to the island. The cool breeze was refreshing as we crossed the lake. We went on several rides and walked around the island. All the day trips were full of fun and food.

So, when negative thoughts flash across my mind, I concentrate on my blessings and all the good times I have experienced. After all, I am still alive. That in itself is a huge blessing. Do I have a good quality of life, considering I have multiple handicaps? That depends on what one's concept of quality of life is. Many people may think I do not. But that does not matter. What matters is how I feel. And yes, I think I have a good quality of life.

I am generally independent, even though I still require medical supervision. I can communicate. I can even cook! I am being trained to become totally independent and I know I will, but not with my breathing. I may need some mechanical breathing assistance for the remainder of my life. But there are many adults who sleep with the aid of Continuous Positive Airway Pressure (CPAP) machines because they have sleep apnea. Like me, they will need the machines for the rest of their lives. Normal? No, but that's life!

So, travelling the road from the time I was born up to now, I've shown the doctors that being paralysed was reversible. I have proven that being mentally delayed did not prevent me from achieving and enjoying life in my own way. I have shown that being in a coma for twelve days did not end my life; having successive cardiac arrests were not death sentences; having collapsed lungs did not kill me. That is defying the odds.

I had to relearn simple things with each setback. I was surrounded by patient and understanding people who showed me how to do so. It took work, creativity and different techniques, but it feels good to know that I was able to bounce back each time. I did it with God's help, together with the guidance and support of caring people.

Even better is being able to write about these deep and personal experiences.

Chapter 5

Comatose and Back

Talk about a cycle. I went from paralysis to walking, from walking to a loss of muscle tone and back to walking again. Thank God I do not have any memory of that time, but my parents explained to me what happened.

When my mom was working on her book, *For a Breath of Life,* I helped with the editing. I remember reading the chapter captioned "Air Ambulance" and could not believe what she had written. I waited until the book was published to ask my questions.

One evening after dinner I joined my parents in the family room. My mom found it strange because Lisaan and I usually head to our rooms to do homework.

"What's up?" my mom questioned.

I am pretty sure she felt I had an assignment to do and needed some assistance.

"That Trinidad trip has me confused. How did I get so sick so quickly?"

"Wait a second, son," my father interrupted. "It was not that Trinidad trip. You began getting sick in Guyana."

When I was two-and-a-half years old, my parents took me to Trinidad and Guyana to see relatives. I heard everyone was happy to see me. My mom's extended family is huge and my problems at birth had everyone anxious.

"Your father is right. Your temperature spiked when we were in Guyana. We immediately took you to grandma's family doctor and he prescribed antibiotics," my mom recalled.

"I realized your condition could get worse, so I headed to the nearest travel agency to book the next flight to Trinidad. The first available reservation was three days later," my dad continued.

As I looked at their faces, I saw the pain they were experiencing. The memory was fresh even though so many years had gone by.

"We had no choice but to wait," my mom said. "Your condition became worse. The day we travelled your breathing was showing signs of trouble. The air pressure in the cabin affected your breathing even more."

"Then what did you do?" I asked.

"We just had to wait out the trip. Once in Trinidad, we spent the night at Auntie Ishra's," my dad added. "The next morning you were looking terrible and your breathing was very shallow."

My parents and Auntie Ishra took me to a doctor in the area. They were told to take me to the hospital. The word went out to all the relatives and just about everyone showed up at the hospital.

"By the time you were admitted you were frothing, grey and lifeless. The doctors gave you oxygen and you started looking better," my mom recalled. "But that was short-lived and before the end of the night you were in the intensive care at the Port-of-Spain General Hospital. And in a coma."

I could not understand what had happened to me, and my parents read my mind.

"What brought on your problem was just a regular cold that developed into pneumonia," my dad informed me. "And you know your breathing is quite delicate."

"But why didn't you use the respirator?"

"At that time you were able to breathe on your own for a three-week period. You would get a boost for a night and then be fine again," my mom explained. "We got permission from the doctors at Sick Kids to take you to Trinidad and Guyana without the respirator. I guess no one expected you to get so sick."

During that conversation I learned about two doctors who cared for me while I was in Trinidad. My parents talk so much about them. Dr. Phyllis Pitt-Miller and Dr. David Bratt could not have done more. They did not have too much hope for me. But, like my doctors in Toronto, they did not give up. To keep me alive, those doctors had to ventilate me by sending tubes down my nostrils. They sent me back to Toronto in an Air Ambulance. I was still in a coma.

My parents accompanied me on that flight. My blood pressure began to drop and the pilot had to make an emergency landing in Miami. The doctors there could not help, so with little hope, the plane was airborne again.

When the plane landed in Toronto, Dr. Edmonds was at the airport and he whisked me away in an ambulance to Sick Kids. An assessment was made on my condition and the results were grim. I was doing no breathing on my own and there were no signs that I would ever be able to do so. My parents were given two options. One was to have surgery and insert a tube in my trachea and the other, to pull the plug. Even though they were against the surgery, they felt it was their only choice.

When I came out of the coma after eleven days, I had lost all my muscle tone and had to learn to walk and talk again. That must have been very hard on my parents. They had taught me to walk and talk once before, and now had to do it all over again.

Nine years after I made my first trip to Trinidad. We visited Dr. Bratt at his office to express our gratitude for all the work he did. He was shocked to see me standing and told my parents that he often wondered what became of me. He also indicated that he never thought that I would have survived when he placed me in the ambulance at Port-of-Spain General Hospital. That visit started a relationship between our families and today, Dr. Bratt is like a member of my mom's family. Whenever I visit Trinidad, I try to see him. Dr. Pitt-Miller is employed at the medical faculty at the University of the West Indies in Trinidad. I have been fortunate to see her a few times. My parents always remind me about their dedication to my care. How lucky I was to have those two on my side!

Chapter 6
Twenty-Five Cents

Why not one cent, five cents or even a dollar? Why twenty-five cents? Why not more? It should have been. Those questions had me digging deep to get the answers, but nothing satisfied me. So like always, I went to my source, my parents, to solve the mystery of the twenty-five cents.

It was a December day. The ground was covered with a fresh snowfall, a sight I love looking at. So clean and untouched. The trees seemed dead without the leaves, but the snow became alive and began to blow with the gusts of the wind. It had to be bitterly cold with those strong winds.

My mom made me a cup of hot chocolate, the perfect drink for the weather. As I sat munching on my toast and sipping my drink, I looked across the table at my mom. She too, was enjoying the wintry landscape. She turned to me with a questioning face and quietly muttered something. I was so engrossed with my twenty-five cents thought that I did not hear what she said. Startled, I sheepishly asked, "What did you say?"

"I thought your mind was elsewhere. What are you thinking about?"

"Oh, this may sound crazy, but my mind is on that twenty-five cents."

"What twenty-five cents?"

"I had read in your book that I was sold to Auntie Ishra."

"Oh, that! What about that twenty-five cents?"

"Well," I timidly continued, "why did you sell me? Didn't you and Dad want me?"

"We still have you, don't we? So it's not because we didn't want you."

"So, what was the big deal in selling me for a lousy quarter?"

"Get one thing straight—there was no deal."

I was becoming agitated and began stuttering. My mom realized her answers were evasive and not what I expected. I had read this part of my mom's book over and over, and it really troubled me. It never made any sense!

"Listen," she said firmly, "that was done when you were a baby and very, very sick. The doctors had told us you would not live. When your great-grandmother in Trinidad heard that, she suggested we sell you to a family member who did not have children."

"Who was the great grandmother?"

"She was Grandpa's mother, my paternal grandmother. So Auntie Ishra relayed the message when she visited Canada the year after you were born. You were about eight months old at the time and still very ill."

I was confused. The explanation still did not make sense to me. Auntie Ishra is my mom's cousin. My mom and her sisters and Auntie Ishra and her sisters are like real sisters. They are so close. Whenever I go to Trinidad on a vacation, both families get together very often. I have problems understanding that relationship. But my mom says they have always shared a very close bond.

I had the opportunity to share some of that love and closeness during my vacations in Trinidad. The first time I visited, they had a get-together and the evening ended with music and dancing. Because of my leg length discrepancy and poor balance, I never ventured on the dance floor. Well, Yassy pulled me up, held my hands for support, and had me moving to the beautiful sound of pan. We danced and danced and I truly enjoyed myself that night. I had a blast.

"I am glad it was Auntie Ishra who bought me, but for twenty-five cents? Couldn't she afford more?"

"Remember this buying story was just a custom."

"I still don't get it though. What was the reason for the sale?"

My mom smiled. She felt the way my question was posed made the entire process sound like a transaction. She looked outside and watched the snow. Huge flakes began falling and the wind was blowing them around.

Suddenly she sighed, breaking the silence between us.

"The sale was made because my grandmother grew up knowing that when a very sick child was sold, he or she had a better chance of survival."

"So, it was really a custom?"

"Oh, yes. I believe it was a cultural practice, which our forefathers brought with them from India. And since you were so ill and the doctors couldn't do anything else for you, your father and I agreed that it wouldn't hurt to fulfill my grandmother's wish. We were prepared to try anything within reason to help you get better. We were desperate."

The custom made absolutely no sense to me then, and it still does not. I am not sure whether it made sense to my parents. All I know is that they wanted me alive.

"But, Mom, why did Auntie Ishra pay just twenty-five cents? That was a rip-off. You know, I feel I am worth more than that."

"And you are," my mother responded. "It was not a matter of the amount of money. It was just symbolic. Auntie Ishra could have given one penny and it would have been fine. The important thing was to hand you over to Auntie Ishra after she gave me the coin."

"You know something, Mom? This whole thing is really sense-less. But, I am still here today. It makes me wonder if the transaction made so many years ago had anything to do with me being alive today. I'm not normal and healthy but I'm still around."

My mom did not think too much about the sale. She could not see how that would cure me or even make me better. Since it was something that did not involve pain, both she and my dad agreed to it.

Perhaps we should all look at customs with some seriousness. Who knows? They can make a difference. I could not have been sold to a better person than Auntie Ishra. She is very special to me. I still wonder, though, why twenty-five cents and not a dollar or more.

That snowy morning certainly set the scene for a cosy conversation. I cleared up an issue that had weighed on my mind for many years. I am happy that my parents did not give me away in the sale. But if they had, my cousin Issa, who lives with Auntie Ishra, would have been my brother. That would have been cool because Issa and I share a very special bond.

Chapter 7

My Lifeline

Night-time, bedtime, sleep time. How I fear that time! It is the most dreaded time of my day. As the daylight fades, my anxiety starts to mount. I wonder why night has to come. I wonder why I have to sleep. Yes, I need rest to function the next day, but why do I have to go to bed with that gruesome machine? I know I will have to use it in the years to come. Any way I look at it, the chances are slim that I will be able to breathe on my own when I go to bed. I will always need some form of ventilation.

Before I settle down at night, I have a routine. Not the changing of clothes or the brushing of teeth. No, those are normal things. First, I have to give a good hard cough and bring up whatever mucus there is in my lungs. Even if I do not need to cough, I force a big one. Sometimes, nothing comes out, and I try again. Just imagine having a cold and coughing often. I've heard a normal person experiences some discomfort and pain. Now think about the constant discomfort I am in. Coughing aches so much I sometimes try to avoid doing it. But the mucus builds up and my breathing becomes laboured, so I need to get rid of it.

After that, I change my trache tube. I have two of them, one for use during the day and the other at night. The night tube has a long piece at the top that is connected to the respirator. When I was younger, my parents changed the tubes for me. My dad tucked me in and prayed over me at night for many years.

As I grew older I became more independent and began doing those things myself. I then flick the main switch at the back of the respirator to the "on" position and connect the tube from the respirator to the tube in my trache. I settle myself in bed and then activate the switch at the front of the respirator.

Swish! The first blast of air goes into my lungs. It feels cold inside, even in the summer. That first blast makes me shiver. Most nights I fall asleep on my side. I can move on my bed, but it means the extra tubing moves also. When I was younger, I slept on my back all the time. Even though my parents told me I could turn, I was afraid to do so. Over the years, I have learned how to turn, and yes, my tubing becomes disconnected at times. When that happens, the respirator alarm wakes me up, along with the rest of the house. My parents get up. To date, they still do not enjoy a full night's sleep. I am not a baby where they have to get up every time they hear a noise. Nor do they have a monitor in their room. Their ears are just automatically tuned in to my alarm, my coughs, my sneezes and my turns.

The alarm goes off whenever there is a problem. If the pressure drops or increases, the alarm will sound. When I cough, the alarm will sound. Just imagine what happens when I have an infection. I think I get more sleep than my parents. When water from the humidifier gets in the tube, the alarm beeps. Power cuts, rate changes, or any malfunction of the respirator will trigger the alarm. That beeping, nagging sound! But what can I do? The respirator is my lifeline. It has kept me alive over the years.

Should my parents have pulled the plug? The doctors asked them when I was extremely ill. And they said yes, on two separate occasions, after much thought. They always asked for time, though, at least one week after giving the okay. On both occasions my parents felt that my quality of life would be poor if I had survived. Each time I began improving before the week was finished. So I never gave the doctors the chance to do one of the hardest things their jobs require them to do. I know my parents made those life-wrenching decisions in my best interest. They did not wish to see me suffer. However, I am not going that easily—not me. I love life too much and what is more important, I think I am here for a purpose.

What will happen if I get married? Like most young men, I have the desire to get married, but many things would stand in my way. One strike against me is my multiple disabilities. Then I have the respirator to consider. How romantic would it be to be hooked up to breathing equipment and sleeping next to my wife? She would have to be very special to agree to such an arrangement. But there are many able-bodied people who sleep with the aid of respirators, so there may be hope for me.

While getting married is very important to me, I have to be practical. It hurts to know I may never get to that stage and enjoy the kind of relationship I see my parents have. I always dreamed of being married by the age of twenty-five. I am older than that, and it pains me deep down to think it may not happen.

Is there a chance I may be able to sleep without the respirator? No. There is nothing in the future yet. Someone will have to come up with an invention before I can get rid of the respirator.

Some children have had success using the Bi-level Positive Air Pressure (BiPap) machine. Others use phrenic pacing or negative pressure ventilation. All of those could replace my trache. The only one left for me to try, however, is phrenic pacing and my parents are now focusing on this option. I hope some research and findings on nerve regeneration will one day solve my breathing problem.

In fact, a few years ago there was a positive breakthrough. I read that Christopher Reeve, the *Superman* actor who was paralyzed in a fall from a horse, was doing some breathing on his own before he died. So I may some day benefit from all the work being done. I may still get the chance to share my love with that special someone!

Chapter 8

Ondine's Curse

Over the years I have had six operations. I remember one specifically, in which I experienced a lot of pain. That was when the doctor had to stop the growth on my right leg and lengthen the muscles in the other. Both legs were in casts. I felt like an invalid. I did not stay in bed, though. I also had my school nurse with me. In fact, I had a nurse with me all the time in public (elementary) and high school. Whenever I was ill and had to be at home, she was assigned to assist my mom in caring for me there.

As I entered my teenage years, I had one wish. I wanted to have my trache removed. It was more for social reasons. The tube is visible and since mucus builds up in my lungs, the frequent coughing can be disgusting. Sometimes the area around the tubes is moist, which then turns crusty. So it's not a very pleasant sight. All of my doctors knew about my wish, but they also realized I would always need some form of ventilation.

My favourite doctor, John Edmonds from The Hospital for Sick Children, agreed to remove the tube after conducting many tests. He just took the tube out and the hole was sealed in a few days. It was odd not having it and I was scared. But I was too macho to say anything. The doctors observed me for a few days, checked to make sure my oxygen level was normal and the carbon dioxide was not accumulating in the body. Feeling satisfied that I was coping, I was discharged from the hospital. It did not mean I was ventilator-free. I still needed non-invasive ventilation via the BiPap machine. It meant wearing a mask over my nose and being ventilated through it rather than the trache. I hated it, but I was prepared to do anything to get rid of the tube.

Two weeks. That was my experience, as far as I can remember, without my trache. It was good but very stressful. I realized I was struggling. Imagine thinking before taking every breath! It was a deliberate effort. I just could not go on. I needed help and quickly. I told my mom how I was feeling and she immediately called Dr. Edmonds. We rushed to The Hospital for Sick Children and to my disappointment, surgery had to be performed to reinsert the tube. That was hell. Nobody could hear my voice after the operation because the tube was preventing air from coming out. So I had to block the hole in the tube with one of my fingers and talk. But even then my voice was only a whisper. How I hated what was happening to me. I ended up writing what I wanted to say. Was I mad at the world then! I wondered whether I would ever be able to be heard again. Had I made the right decision to admit I was experiencing respiratory difficulty? My other choice would have been death. Still, nobody could have said anything to make me feel better.

I was frustrated, angry, helpless and dejected. Those emotions were evident. I was too young to remember anything that happened the first time I had the trache. I was only two-and-a-half years old. The second time around, at the age of sixteen, I was old enough to remember everything and felt the physical and mental anguish. The nurses had to deep suction me. What a horrible experience! I gagged and choked each time the suction tube went down into my lungs.

I felt defeated. I lost all hope. My mom continued sending the tubes down my trachea after I was discharged from the hospital. I cannot imagine how she felt knowing she was making me gag and choke. At the time I felt if I could see the doctor who was responsible for injuring me at birth, I would tell him where the hell to go. I despised him for doing what he did to me. I cried. Tears streamed down my face frequently. I even hated the nurses then. I knew they suctioned me so I could breathe better, but that feeling was awful.

In my mom's book, *For a Breath of Life*, she wrote that I kicked up a storm when I was a fetus. If I moved so much, what happened? Common sense tells me a moving fetus cannot end up being a paralysed baby! Unless, of course, something went wrong. How I wish the doctor who delivered me could explain that one. I know doctors are human beings. And I also know that to err is human. How I would love to meet with him face-to-face so he could explain to me what he did or did not do. I am pretty sure I would not understand everything, but I would be happy just hearing the explanation straight from the horse's mouth. Not knowing why I am being punished this way is not fair. I am being punished for something I did not do. I look at my friends and wonder why I have to be the way I am. No one can explain my condition to me. If the doctor will not tell me, then my only choice will be to ask my Maker when I face him someday.

Initially, I needed the respirator twenty-four hours a day. Now I need it only at nights and during the day when I have a severe infection. My gait is still not normal and I do not think it will ever become normal.

Is there anything normal with me? I have to think for a moment. I can hear. I can see. For that, I am thankful. I can eat independently. For that I am grateful because I love to eat. I am mobile with limitations, yet another gift. I can smell and touch. My five senses are intact. Wow! I have so much to be thankful for. So yes, there are things I can do. I can bathe myself but still need help to wash my hair and cut my nails. Goodness, the things we take for granted! While others may look at me differently, I feel I am normal in my own way. It really comes down to a person's thinking.

My birth injury left me with specific limitations. The doctor who delivered me used forceps to take me out of the birth canal. From what I read in my mom's book, it seemed I needed help to be born. So the obstetrician, trying to do his job, realized I needed some assistance. He clamped my head with the forceps, twisted it into position and yanked me out. That was some "good delivery"! Did he twist my head too much? I even wonder whether he pulled me too hard.

Grey, lifeless and silent, I entered the world. Some brain damage occurred because I did not get oxygen fast enough. My breathing went berserk from the time I was born. Not being able to breathe and move on my own created problems. If monitors were connected to my mom, surely the doctor would know things were not happening the way they should. Why did he wait so long? He should have made decisions earlier. I was a full-term baby and weighed seven pounds, ten ounces, according to my parents. My problems could have started in the birth canal, and the doctor realizing this and in his anxiety to help, did more harm than good.

I was sent to The Hospital for Sick Children, where I remained for more than one year. Because of the lack of oxygen during my early life, I am slow. In every area I experience frustration. I would like to live the life of a so-called normal human being for a few days just to see what it feels like. And yes, I would also like an able-bodied person to live in my shoes for a few days.

The medical staff at the hospital gained a great deal of knowledge caring for me. I was a tough patient, tough in the sense that the doctors were trying everything they knew. They probably thought I had potential, so they kept on trying. I guess they also saw the commitment from my parents, who visited every day and spent so many hours bonding with me. I'm sure glad they all worked hard and I improved to the point where I was able to walk and breathe independently during the day.

By now you must be wondering about the nature of my medical condition, the condition that made my life a living hell. So it is time to give it a name. When I was old enough to question my parents about the illness, I did not learn much and quickly realized there was not a great deal doctors knew about it. Very casually, I asked my mom one day. She told me it was called Ondine's Curse.

"How could it be a curse? Did someone put a curse on me? What is Ondine's Curse?" I asked.

I guess she herself did not know how to explain the weird condition. She was stumped. If you know my mom, being at a loss for words is rare for her. I chuckled inside because I knew she just did not know where to begin. I had caught her off guard.

Hesitantly, she began, "Not much is really known about the illness. I have explored different avenues to learn whatever I could, but there is not much out there. But I am sure no one has put a curse on you."

"Then why would it be referred to as a curse?"

"Well, there was a Greek goddess called Ondine and she—"

"Wait, wait, what does a goddess have to do with my problems?" I interrupted.

"Hear me out and then you can continue." she added.

"Ondine was married to a mortal, but he was unfaithful and she placed a curse on him. The curse stopped all his automatic functions. So, when her husband fell asleep, he stopped breathing and died."

"Then Ondine was a mean and nasty lady," I stated.

"You can say so, but remember that is a myth. However, there are different mythological interpretations, but I know you want to know more from a medical standpoint."

"Yes, Mom," I responded, anxiously. "After all, I am living the curse."

"Well, Ondine's Curse has many different names. It is referred to as Central Hypoventilation Syndrome, Idiopathic Hypoventilation, or Congenital Central Alveolar Hypoventilation."

Listening to all those big names confused me even more. I decided to stick with Ondine's Curse. As horrible as it sounded, it was much easier for me to remember. My mom also told me there were only a few people in the world with the condition. At the time of my birth, there were about forty recorded cases. From the latest medical information my mom received, there are now about one hundred and ninety-six known cases.

I always knew I was different, but *that* different? My poor doctors did not have a clue what to do with me. They were at a loss on how to treat me. Sometimes, upon reflection, I wish God did not choose me. Then, on second thought, I figured if he did not choose me, he would have chosen another child. I am very fortunate to have parents who sacrificed their time and careers for my well-being. Maybe, if God had chosen another child for this condition, he or she might not have been as lucky.

My education on Ondine's Curse continued. It is a neurological damage to the brain stem. The brain stem is the base of the brain. Any damage to that part of the brain affects breathing. During the day my breathing is normal. Once I fall asleep, however, my muscles relax too much and my breathing becomes shallow. As a result, the message to tell me to breathe does not go to the brain fast enough. Because my brain was damaged during delivery, I acquired the disease.

My cousin Nadeem, who lives in Trinidad, started medical school in 2001 and he told me one of his friends in a senior year had an exam on respiration. They were discussing that topic and my cousin talked about my condition. He said his friend became curious and began questioning him. Eventually, the name Ondine's Curse came out. Obviously, his friend had never heard of it, and they both checked their medical texts and found a few lines on the topic. The student opened his exam the following day, and to his surprise, one of the questions was on Ondine's Curse. Nobody in the class, except that young man, was able to answer the question accurately. The young man thanked Nadeem for enlightening him on Ondine's Curse. So, my condition continues to provide knowledge to others. I have helped my doctors, nurses, teachers, psychologists, my parents, and a young man who is aspiring to become a doctor. Life is worth living! I am convinced that my purpose in life is to educate and inspire people by sharing my experiences.

For most of my childhood and teenage life, I have been sick. Chest infections progressed to pneumonia on many occasions. A lot of times I needed the respirator to help with my breathing during the day. I dislike sleeping with that machine, especially during the day, but what other choice do I have? Every time I have to be attached to it during the day, I feel defeated. I need it when I have a severe chest infection, but it is so demoralizing to give in. Whenever I go to Trinidad on vacation, I have to get a one-hour boost during the day because of the heat and humidity. I hate that with a passion. But the heat tires me. Without the boost from my respirator, I would not be able to enjoy the vacation. My resistance would become lower and lower and eventually I could get very sick.

I missed a lot of school. If my mom was not there to teach me, I would not have been able to do as well as I did. Doing research while lying on a hospital bed was a regular for me. My mom took encyclopedias for me to gather the necessary information to complete my projects. Most times, my nurses, Angela and Ron, would pick up my assignments from school and drop them off for me.

My entire life has been about seeing specialists. Respirologists, neurologists, ophthalmologists, cardiologists, urologists—you name the "ologist," and I have likely seen one. Being stuck with needles and IVs, having X-rays, cardiograms, MRIs, cat scans, sleep studies, antibiotics, and puffs are all part of life for me.

These doctors have kept me alive, doctors just like the one who delivered me. Each one specialized in a different field. I am upset with the one who delivered me, but grateful to those who have tried and are still trying to help me.

Very often I sit back and wonder what my life would have been like if nothing had happened to me. I imagine myself as a normal, healthy young man. Maybe I would have given my parents different types of problems. I might have been on drugs or alcohol. I might be out partying at nights, or, like my sister, I might have been a top-notch student and a role model for others. I would not have been home often. My favourite place might have been pubs or bars. I think my father would have freaked out!

People ask me all the time if I want to become a doctor. I always answer in the negative, and tell them that while I have learned a lot of medical terminology and seen tons of medical equipment through my years, the medical field does not interest me at all. It is too dangerous and risky for me, as the lives of people are at stake. Even if I wanted to become a doctor, it is difficult to say whether my brain would enable me to absorb, remember and fully practise all that medical knowledge. Keep in mind my brain still does not function as well as it should. I would not like to live with the guilt of causing another human being the pain and trauma I've had to endure.

From paralysis to walking, from being ventilated twenty-four hours a day to night-time only, from living as a vegetable to a functioning human being, I am a person—one who has overcome a hell of a lot, wrestling with the goddess Ondine to become the individual I am today!

Chapter 9
My First Vacation

My family went nine long years without a vacation. After that dreadful experience when I was two-and-a-half years old, my parents were scared to board a plane. They were afraid the same thing would happen again—a reasonable fear.

But something had to put an end to that. Someone did some serious talking and convincing before my parents carefully took the first step. My aunt invited us to spend a few days in Orlando, Florida.

"Orlando!" I exclaimed. "Geez. How exciting!"

"Don't build your hopes up," my mom halted my excitement. "Auntie Baby was very kind to extend an invitation for us to stay in her family's condo, but we have a lot of things to sort out before considering such a huge undertaking."

All the necessary arrangements were made: permission to fly, to take the respirator on board, letters from doctors at Sick Kids and an emergency contact in Florida. I could not believe the things that had to be done. It took quite a few days for arrangements to be finalized. Then came the packing. My mom listed the medical equipment that I would need. She included extra supplies in case of emergency. We all had carry-on luggage—medical supplies only.

I was excited and could not control my emotions. I was going to Orlando. Disney World! That was the only thing on my mind.

We boarded the plane and I could feel the thrill. My parents had to buckle my seat belt since it was the first plane ride I could remember. So they gave me a lesson on how to do the task. My sister was quite cool and knew what to do because she spent about five summers in Trinidad.

The attendant announced the departure, and as we were airborne, I began feeling uncomfortable but did not say anything. My dad looked at me and asked if I was relaxed. I nodded.

"How are your ears?" he inquired.

"Why?"

"They should be getting blocked up."

I immediately settled down, realizing that my experience was normal.

"Just swallow when you feel the pressure building in your ear. It will stop shortly."

I was bored during the flight. We had refreshments and I spent most of the time doing crossword puzzles. After a few hours, the attendant announced that we were close to Orlando and asked us to buckle up again. We landed safely and my excitement returned. My parents waited until everyone left the plane, then gathered our belongings and headed to the terminal. As we were going down the escalator, I noticed two people at the bottom.

No, it can't be, I thought. I shook my head and blinked my eyes. I looked again and saw the same two people. *Uh-uh! It can't be*. I knew I was seeing them, but in Orlando?

"Yassy and Teen!" I screamed. "Yeah-h-h-h!" They had smiles on their faces. My aunts Yassy (Yasmin) and Teen (Shereen) are my mom's sisters. They knew they had surprised my sister and me! My parents were aware of their plans. We were also met at the airport by my dad's sister, Mezaun and her husband, Alan, and spent the first night with them.

The next day we went to the condo and quickly settled in. My parents rented a van and shopped for groceries. We were ready to holiday and I could not wait. Yassy insisted that we go to Disney first. We bought a four-day pass. What fun Disney was!

We crammed a lot of things into our week-long vacation, but my most memorable moments were at Disney World and Universal Studios. Magic Kingdom was my favourite. It was truly magic! I enjoyed all the rides especially *It's a Small World*. The music on each ride was so relaxing. I enjoyed seeing Goofy, Minnie Mouse and all those characters. It was like a dream.

I did not enjoy Epcot Centre too much. That was a lot of science for me, but my parents loved that.

The real highlight of the holiday was when we went to MGM (Metro Goldwyn Mayer) Studios. We were present for the taping of "Let's Make a Deal," and my dad was selected to be one of the participants. It was hilarious to see him dressed as a sailor. I was thrilled at just being in the audience. I love to watch game shows on television and being at a live taping was out of this world. My dad did not win any of the grand prizes, but he came away with one Disney Dollar. Despite that, he still had a good time.

We ate out a lot during the vacation. Lunch and dinner were at restaurants. That I enjoyed. Food is one of my pastimes and I ate my fill. We usually ate breakfasts at home. We had very long days, leaving our condo after breakfast and returning late at night.

I remained healthy throughout the week. I was sorry the vacation had to end. My aunts left and returned to Trinidad and we headed back to cold Toronto. That vacation gave my parents some hope that I could venture farther than Orlando. My mom felt we could consider trips to Trinidad as a family.

So, Orlando was not only fun and adventurous, but it was also breaking the ice for me to travel more.

Chapter 10

Education

Brain-damaged, mentally retarded, slow learner, multiple handicapped. If words could kill, I would be dead today. I have heard those words repeatedly and some I've seen written in many reports during my school years.

Yet, today I am a graduate of Seneca College, where I completed a two-year program in radio broadcasting in 2002. I graduated with honours, and I'm very proud of my accomplishment.

While shopping one day, I met one of my public school friends, John. We stood and talked for a while and he was thrilled when I told him I graduated from college.

"You graduated from college? And in radio too? Wow!" He was unable to contain his excitement. The last he had heard was that colleges had turned down my applications.

"Didn't you tell me at one point you were not supposed to walk or talk?" he sarcastically asked.

"Yeah, that's what I was told, but you can't believe everything you hear," I pointed out.

"Good thing you never believed what you were told. I'm very, very happy for you," he continued.

"You know how much I had to rack my brains to reach this point? It was tough."

"So we'll have to listen out for you now."

"That is if I get a job. You know it won't be easy for me. Right now, I'm sending out resumes to radio and television stations," I informed him.

John boosted my ego when he said, "We always knew you had the will. You did us proud, bro."

"Thanks, man. I wish all my teachers in public and high school could see me now. Remember when I was in that class where all I did was make beds and go bowling and swimming? That made me mad because I was never taught anything constructive. Thank God my parents fought to get me out of there."

During the few years when I was in that class, I was never really interested in learning. The teacher made me feel I could never learn, so I never showed I could. Based on the academic assessments, she probably felt that I could not, and I do not blame her. She did what was expected of her. My mom worked with me at home and she always told me I was capable, so my work habits were different at home. It is amazing the effect that people's expectations have on you. Even we challenged people sense it.

"Do you remember when I told you about that teacher who put me out of the music class?" I asked John.

"Yeah man, how could I forget. She was mean. I still can't understand why she did that. She knew you had a breathing problem and she wanted you to play the recorder. After all, it doesn't take a genius to know it would be tough. Even us kids knew that."

No one really understood how humiliated I felt that day. My feelings were hurt and my confidence was shattered. I was insulted in front of my classmates. How could an educated person expect me to play a recorder, an activity that entails controlled breathing? I sat outside the classroom like a lost dog. Some students thought I was just too dumb to play the instrument. Some turned around and made fun of me. But there were some who were kind and courteous. My heart was crying, but no tears fell from my eyes. I was beaten down yet again.

Luckily, I have the ability to pull myself up very quickly. I went into the "I can" mode my parents instilled in me at an early age. I have been taught that I can do anything I set my mind to do. However, setting my mind is one thing; working hard to achieve it is another. I must show initiative, be responsible and persevere. Working hard never got rid of the hurt I experienced, but accomplishing a goal always made me feel better about myself and increased my confidence.

Teachers play a very important role in the lives of children. Yet, a few choose to show no compassion whatsoever. If teachers can be so cruel, what do they expect from children? I was determined to show my teacher and my classmates that I could play the recorder like everyone else, despite my disabilities and the humiliation. With assistance from my mom, who coached me for hours, I proudly stood in front of the class the next day and delivered a piece that shocked the teacher. Boy, did I enjoy looking at her expression. I still smile when I think about it, even today. It was not easy for me to control my breathing. It took long hours of practice, but I was not prepared to give in until I got it right. I am pretty sure my mom was exhausted. Imagine blowing into the recorder and having some the air come out through my trache tube. Some of the air was going into the instrument to help create the sound and some was escaping. I was tired. But by the time I was finished late at night, I felt confident.

During my school life, I tried to get involved in a few extracurricular activities. It meant sacrificing some of my lunch hour and remaining in school after the bell sounded at three o'clock. It was the first term of the school year, (1991) and the Christmas concert was approaching. I decided to join the choir. I was accepted in the choir and I felt really good about myself. Shortly after, the pressure started to build. Although I was not told directly about my voice, I knew comments the teacher made in practice referred to me. After the concert, she told me that she did not think it was wise for me to remain in the choir because I was not attending practices regularly. I felt like punching her for doing what she did to me. I later learned she told others my voice was throwing the other students off-key.

I sat and thought about my life. How would I ever get ahead when people just continue to throw obstacles in my way? I was helpless and hurt. I was screaming inside, "O God, help me! Help me deal with this! Am I that bad? The rejection is too much to handle." It took some time to calm myself. But I decided to continue on, confront my obstacles and deal with them as they came.

Despite all the humiliation, I received an award for determination and perseverance when I graduated from public school. I was surprised, but it felt great to be acknowledged.

Over the years I met some very caring, kind, considerate and patient teachers. In fact, most of my teachers were excellent. It reminds me of a bag of potatoes. Most of them are good, but there are times where you find the odd one that is not as good. At every level of my education, I met teachers who showed how much they cared and they helped erase the negative comments I received from others. My parents described the good teachers as angels.

My first angel was Mrs. Kim Smith, in public school. She showed me that I had potential. She felt the way my parents did, and she encouraged me. She was kind and very soft-spoken. With her encouragement, I wrote my first book. It was only eight pages, but it was an accomplishment. She was the one who had me integrated into the mainstream classes. I was scared stiff the first day, but she believed in me and wanted better for me. Mrs. Smith is now a principal at another public school.

My second angel was Mrs. Bev Carson. She was my special education teacher in secondary school. Mrs. Carson continued where Mrs. Smith left off and my parents were very happy that someone else showed interest. She helped whenever I experienced difficulties and always offered words of encouragement. I was sad she retired before I finished high school. She would have assisted me in my fight to do Writer's Craft. This course was designed for students who wanted to further develop their writing skills.

That was one time I cried in high school. Imagine being told you cannot do something without having the chance to attempt it. I was told the subject, Writer's Craft would be too difficult. I failed without writing a word! But I begged and begged and finally got the chance to participate. And when I did, I passed the subject! Why did I have to feel I was not good enough? Why did I have to feel rejected? Mrs. Carson would not have allowed me to fight the battle alone. She would have spared me the pain and trauma, offering support every step of the way.

My third angel was Jim Carr, who taught me in college. It did not take him long to realize I was there to succeed. The best thing about him was that he was really cool. He treated his students as adults and expected us to assume responsibility for our academic progress.

Other teachers were also great, but I chose to mention just one from every level of my education. Each one I mentioned showed personal interest in my education. I suppose they knew I worked hard, had very good family support and tried my best even when the work was difficult. They were always there to lend a hand. It would have been difficult to survive if I did not have them around to turn to when the going got tough.

I cannot process information quickly, so teaching me required a lot of patience. Memorizing facts requires constant repetition.

There were times when I wanted to close the books for good. Simple things seemed like trigonometry to me. And yes, I also did trigonometry. How far-fetched that was! I can remember my mom doing math with me one day. She put a simple addition into a problem-solving form. Not for the life of me could I figure out what to do. I just could not understand the problem. Once it was solved, I was fine. Imagine at the age of nine having difficulty solving something like: Matt went to the store with $5.00. He bought a newspaper for $1.25 and a candy bar for $.79. How much change did he get? That was like Greek to me. The Greek goddess made me wrestle with the process.

At the time, I could not understand why I had difficulty grasping simple concepts. I became frustrated trying and trying. I would look at my sister and see how easily she would absorb information. My mom gave me other problems, changing only the numbers and I was still lost. When problems had two steps, I sat and stared at them.

Learning was a big task. I hated it because it made me feel stupid, as if I would never make it in life. But I put my mind to it and spent hours doing tasks over and over until I got the hang of it. Repetition was the key factor. My mom had to keep repeating things daily. She was so patient. I was truly disgusted hearing the same things over and over, but it was my only hope and it paid off.

So I succeeded in my own way because of great parents, understanding teachers and aunts who showed what good teachers could do. My mom and all her sisters and some of her cousins are teachers. They are obsessed with education just like Grandpa Baksh. In August 2003, Grandpa retired from the Teaching Service Commission in Trinidad and Tobago after spending sixty seven years in the field of education. My mom's family has always shown great interest in my schoolwork. They believed in me, despite my limited capabilities, and they never made me feel left out of anything. My aunts breathe education all the time—a little too much for my liking, though. But it was their dedication and encouragement that gave my mom the strength to work with my low IQ and helped me to succeed.

My education was an ongoing battle. Those who had to recommend my next level of education always wanted to place me with others who were severely mentally challenged. How did these people expect me to improve? I needed to be with children who were brighter. After graduating from public school, it was recommended I attend a special school where I would be at the top of the class. Everyone in the school board probably thought that was where I belonged. But did anyone ever consider asking me? I am happy my parents knew what I wanted for myself and fought the bureaucrats to get what I deserved—integration into the mainstream system!

The integration process was an uphill battle. At the end of every school year, my parents had to attend an Identification Placement and Review Committee (IPRC) meeting. Those present from the Ministry of Education, including my teacher and principal, had to say what was going to happen to me the next year. Throughout public school, those meetings, according to my parents, were always tense. Things became heated at times, with raised voices and tears. My parents wanted one thing and the teachers, with the exception of Mrs. Smith and a few others, wanted something else. But my parents stood firm. I count my lucky stars that my mom knows about education. She knew what she was talking about at those meetings. She was familiar with the terms teachers used and she stood up for me.

My mom was prepared to take the recommendation the panel made in grade eight to the media because a special school was recommended. The consultants from the board asked my parents to give them two weeks. Sure enough, they came back with a positive answer—the school I wanted to attend. Families caring for disabled children are stressed every day. Why put them through more? They should be spared. Their task should be caring for the children, not fighting the bureaucrats!

My parents said that the school board did not accept me in the public school system because of my trache. At that time, no child in the region had a trache tube. So the officials did not know what to do. Arrangements had to be made to have a nurse with me because the school was not equipped to take care of my medical needs. It took my mom about six months, phoning the school board, consultants, the Ministry of Education and the school before I was finally accepted in a Life Skills program. My mom was stressed out after that, but little did she know the battles were only beginning!

High school was another fight. It was not an automatic transition. Some public school teachers felt I did not have the brains to cope with the curriculum in a regular high school. I lost the taxi service provided to children with special needs because I did not accept the special school that was recommended.

Then came college. With seven Ontario Academic Credits, I would be accepted—or so I thought. The colleges turned down my applications. I was devastated. My sister was being accepted at different universities with scholarships and colleges were turning me down. What a low blow. My sister was in a position to make choices and there was none for me. I began to think about what would happen if my education came to a halt. I wondered what my life would be and what kind of a job I would get with only a high school diploma. My dad decided to appeal the decision made by the first college of my choice. My mom was unable to do much because she had just completed her cancer treatment and was coping with the severe side effects.

Dad sent a letter to the president of Seneca College with supporting letters from the guidance counsellor at Markville Secondary and two personal references from very close friends of our family. My mom then made several follow-up calls to the admissions department to ensure our request was being looked into. We also contacted another friend of ours who lectured at Seneca College to see if he could offer any assistance. Dr. Ibrahim Hayani came into our lives after the publication of my mom's book. He contacted us after reading about it in the Toronto Star. Dr. Hayani also approached the college on our behalf.

A hearing was scheduled for my parents and me to attend. What a nerve-racking ordeal! I walked into a room full of adults from different areas of the college. There were senior people from the administration, including the dean of the faculty, the program coordinator and the special needs representative. I froze when I saw all those top people. The butterflies were fluttering in my stomach. My legs felt like a ton of bricks. How would I ever convince those people I was capable of learning?

After we were seated around the table, I listened to all the reasons the educators offered as to why I could not make it in college. *Hell*, I thought, *their minds are already made up! I have to come out and be truly powerful for them to change their minds.* So many people to convince! Was I capable? I had no choice.

Mustering all the courage I had, I pleaded my case. I told the panel I understood their concerns about the amount of time I would have to spend on assignments, about the level of difficulty of the work and my learning disabilities. I ended my plea by saying, "All I am asking for is a chance."

After some discussions, my wish was granted; but like so many times before, I had to prove myself. Certain conditions were laid out.

Every phase of my school life was a hurdle, all because many of those who were in positions to make the decisions made wrong ones—at least for me. I understand my brain does not function normally. And I also know that, based on different assessments, I should not have succeeded. But I did. While the experts think they make decisions in the best interest of the student, more thought should be given to each situation. Maybe another child with the same injury as mine may not have done as well.

If my parents had listened to the educators who had written me off, what type of person would I be today? I shudder to think!

Chapter 11
Social Isolation

While there are tons of activities and opportunities for disabled people, my multiple disabilities prevent me from participating in most.

I do not go out with my friends regularly. What they do in an hour would take me much longer. There was little time for fun during my school years. Yes, I was invited out, but I went only when I did not have assignments with deadlines. Sadly, that was not often. In high school, I made some really genuine friends. Even though I have finished college, those high school friends are still there for me. They understand my shortcomings. They have not forgotten me. They never ignore me or make me feel different. I am not as bright as they are, but they always include me in their group. They ask! They give me the option to say no. And they don't assume that I will not participate.

The staring from people when I am out in public makes me uncomfortable. I am sure that other people with disabilities experience the same thing. The non-disabled have to be conscious of the discomfort their staring causes. Maybe I look like an alien with my trache, but I need it to remain alive. I would feel much better if people would approach me and politely ask, "I'm just curious. What do you have around your neck?" Or, "I don't mean to be nosy, but why are you wearing that around your neck?" If people are informed, they would not have the need to stare.

I remember someone meeting me for the first time and asking if I was trying to start a new fashion trend by wearing that "thing" around my neck. Now, this individual asked and I should have felt good, but I did not. His tone of voice was sarcastic and belittling and made me feel uncomfortable. My dad must have sensed the guy was trying to make fun of me and he really let him have it.

Those of us with disabilities are usually aware of the looks and gazes we get. If we are unaware, those who accompany us pick up on the glances, the smirks, the penetrating eyes, the sneers and glares. People with disabilities have feelings. We are human beings. We are hurt, the same way any normal person is hurt. This not only happens with strangers but also within the family circle and community. I am acknowledged at family and social gatherings, but I can sense the effort it takes for some people to talk to me. Most do it out of duty. During my motivational speaking engagements, I always remind people that anyone can become disabled at any time. Remember, I did not ask to be disabled. Anybody can be the next one chosen. So, have a caring heart. Reach out. Do not exclude, include!

When I began high school, children ignored me. It happened during public school also, but I was younger and it did not bother me as much. As I grew older, I became more aware of it. Each time I felt alone. For a normal teenager, high school can be traumatic. Can you imagine what it was like for me? Well, the isolation became worse. Eventually, one of my teachers called my mom and said, "We seem to be having a social problem with Azeem." My mom was caught by surprise because she knew I was pretty sociable, especially when I am treated with respect and dignity.

"A social problem?" my mom questioned in disbelief. "That's very strange."

Mrs. Carson, my special needs teacher, went on to explain it was isolation by other students, which she suspected was due to a lack of knowledge. "What should we do?" she asked.

"I would suggest you talk to the students and explain the medical condition. If you are not comfortable doing it, I would be more than happy to speak to them," my mom replied.

A date was agreed upon and my mom, being a teacher herself, delivered a very effective and simple presentation. She educated the children about the trache. She informed them it was the only thing keeping me alive. The children gasped when they heard that. They never realized my problems started at birth and that my brain was damaged to the point where I could not breathe.

"This equipment here," my mom said, referring to the suction kit, "is used to extract mucus from Azeem's lungs. It may look like a blue box to you, but it is one of his lifelines. He has to take it with him wherever he goes. When children make fun of him, he avoids using the suction kit and has difficulty breathing. Would you prefer if he stops breathing?" she asked the class.

No, they all shook their heads, too stunned to answer.

"Azeem does not want your sympathy. He wants your friendship. He wants to be accepted for who he is. I want all of you to realize that any one of you can be hit by a car today and become disabled. Would you like to be ignored and isolated? It is always better to be kind and lend a helping hand. Remember, Azeem is a person. He has feelings. He is a teenager, just like you. He likes to hang out and shoot the breeze the same way you do. If you try talking to him, you will find that he enjoys goofing around and has a great sense of humour. All he wants is to be treated with respect."

My mom told me she would always remember a comment one student made during the question-and-answer period. "Mrs. Kayum, you have taught me a lot today. I was one who felt Azeem could not mix. I am happy you came in." That, my mom said, made it all worthwhile.

Being a teenager, I was self-conscious and chose not to go to class that morning. Based on the reaction of the students, I knew some of them felt guilty for ignoring me. Some became very good friends and always looked out for me afterwards. A little education goes a long way.

The isolation continued in a different arena—at college. We were adults then. Who would have thought I would feel so much alone? A big blow came when our first group assignment was given in Radio Programming. I succeeded in finding a group, a miracle for me. However, it was too good to be true. My world was shattered the next day when the others in the group replaced me with someone else. I was devastated, hurt, demoralized, belittled and once again alone and isolated. I was determined not to allow that incident to keep me down permanently, but it was tough trying to be upbeat.

My mom reads me like a book. She sensed something was wrong when she picked me up from college and immediately began her cross-examination.

"What's wrong?" she asked without even saying hello.

"Oh, nothing," I answered, trying to hide my true feelings and remain cool.

"I don't think so," she continued. "I can tell from your expression that something happened. Your shoulders are slouched and you are not your perky self."

"Yep, I'm cool." I lied.

"Can't fool me, you know. Something happened today. I'm waiting to hear."

There was silence in the vehicle, interrupted only by the passing cars and trucks.

"You know I'm not going to leave this alone," my mom insisted.

Hesitantly, I poured my heart out. "Remember the group assignment? Well, one group member kicked me out of the group."

"Don't worry," my mom calmly consoled me. "These things you have to expect and you will continue to face them as long as you live. Keep in mind that these people don't know you and in their eyes you are different." It sounded harsh, but it was so true.

"But it hurts each time," I blurted out.

"I know. These guys don't know better," my mom repeated.

"Shouldn't they, though? They are grown individuals, most in their twenties. How can they be so mean?" I continued, more puzzled than ever.

My mom tried to boost my spirits, but it was tough to feel better. The pain inside me was so great that I wanted to cry and scream but was too embarrassed to do so.

My mom, sensing how hurt I was, interrupted my self-pity. "Well, when is the assignment due?"

"In two weeks."

"The first thing you have to do is e-mail the professor and tell him what happened."

"No way! I can't do that! I have to fix this myself."

"Won't it be better to inform your professor rather than wait? You only have two weeks."

An argument followed because I did not feel I should involve the professor. But arguments are hard to win with my mom, especially when it deals with education. After exchanging opinions, I gave in. Fortunately, prior to my next class, I was able to join a group without the professor's assistance.

Shortly after that incident, the same young man who encouraged the group to kick me out needed help in another class, doing a one-hour broadcast to the school. He actually approached me!

I wondered why he came to me. After all, he did not think I was good enough for his group. My parents always tell my sister and me that we should try to lend a helping hand whenever we can. There are occasions when I disagree with that approach, and this was one of them. I did it anyway. The guy must have been surprised I was willing to assist him. Despite all my weaknesses I also have my strengths and he recognized I had no fears when handling the microphone. I encouraged and provided him with the support he needed.

In one of my other college classes, a different professor gave another group assignment. He named four group leaders and asked each one to pick a student to join his or her group. I was among the last four students left. The professor must have sensed what would have happened, so he assigned each of the remaining four to a group. He came to me after the class to apologize.

"This is not strange. I'm used to it," I lied. No one gets used to isolation and humiliation. But these events don't surprise me. Those people are strangers. However, some family members treat me the same way.

One particularly hurtful event occurred at a family wedding when I was only twelve. All the grandchildren formed the bridal party—with one exception! Guess who? Even my five-year-old cousin was included! So, if my sister and my older and younger cousins were all included, I have to assume it was because of my disabilities that I was left out. I do not think I can describe the deep and piercing pain I felt when I realized I was the *only one* omitted. My stomach was in knots. I believe my parents should not have allowed my sister to be part of the bridal party. Also, my dad was the master of ceremonies for the religious segment of the wedding. In my opinion, he should not have taken such an active role in the proceedings, but he did.

My mom did not say a word, as far as I know. She just allowed the whole thing to happen. I believe that she did not want to create any discord among the family members. I wanted to run far away and cry. I was so shattered. I could not believe that my own relatives would be so unfeeling. I didn't want to be where I was not appreciated.

I wonder sometimes if my relatives thought about how I felt when my sister and all my cousins were going to the rehearsal. Maybe everyone thought I was too brain-damaged and did not have the sense to understand. Little did they know! I understood what was going on. I had always dreamed of riding in a stretch limousine, and this was one opportunity I had to realize this dream, sitting in the stretch with all my cousins. But I was stuck in our van with my mom and dad.

My dad picked up on my sadness and took me to the rehearsal with the hope I would feel better. But it made me feel more isolated. The hurt I felt was no different from other occasions. But this time I was among my own flesh and blood. I was among hundreds of people and yet I was very lonely—and angry.

I do not care to know who was responsible for making the decision to omit me. The damage was done. Were they embarrassed with the way I walk? Would I have made the wedding pictures look terrible? Perhaps seeing me on the video walking with a limp would not look right in their eyes. Now that I am older, I wonder what other family members and friends thought about the situation. For me, it was demeaning and insulting. It was isolation to the highest degree.

Getting through the day took its toll on me. I had to put some of the lessons my parents taught me into practice. One of them was to accept the situation, even though I may not like the events, and appear to be happy. That was extremely tough to do. Mom made sure that I was well taken care of and I sensed that she felt the pain that I was experiencing. Somehow, I was able to get through the day. Here again I believe that God gave me the strength I needed to cope with the isolation and humiliation I faced that day. The ability to deal with a situation like that develops over time. A person must truly believe in himself in order to move on after such a deep hurt.

Accepting people with disabilities is the number one step toward integration. Only then can we move ahead. That acceptance must begin with immediate and extended family. I am an individual who turned out differently. I walk with a slight limp and with one leg kicking out to the side. My speech is sometimes affected. My breathing is the pits. All the jobs that entail processing, co-ordination, motor skills, and comprehension are delayed. But I am a person who senses when he is wanted and appreciated in a place. Those of us with disabilities are blessed with that extra sense.

Make the effort to reach out. Exercise patience. Reflect on my experiences. Make a difference in someone else's life. Put yourself in the shoes of the disabled. Think before you act and speak, and keep in mind you, too, can become disabled in an instant. Disabilities know no limits. They affect even the rich and famous.

When you experience the pangs of isolation and the feeling of being tossed aside, you would not want anyone else to feel excluded. Trust me. I have experienced it time and again. And I know it is something I will have to deal with for the rest of my life. But that can change when normal people make the effort.

By sharing my story, I am hoping for change. You, my friends, can make it happen!

1. Hooked up to a ventilator shortly after birth.

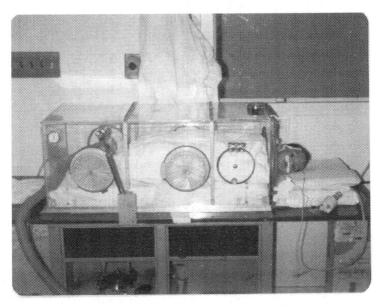

2. In "the box" using negative pressure ventilation.

3. Learning to walk at two.

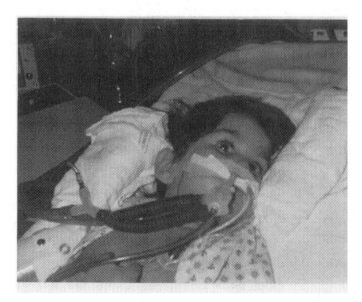

4. At age two-and-a-half.

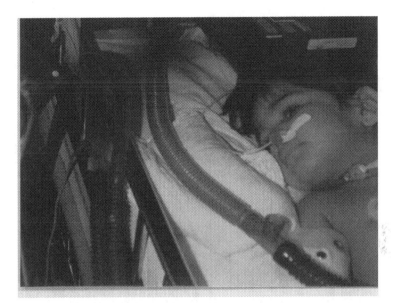

5. With the trache tube in place.

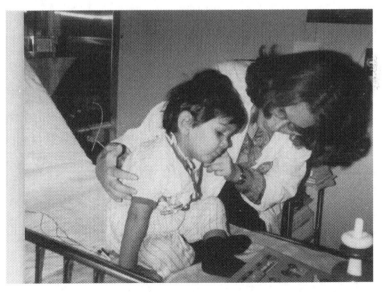

6. Receiving support from Dr. Pape.

7. At home after the trache insertion.

8. A clinical visit with my dad at Sick Kids.

9. After heel cord lengthening.

10. Resting with my sister at Disney World.

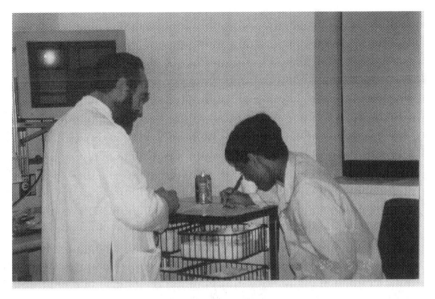

11. Dr. Edmonds looking on as I sign an authorization form for surgery.

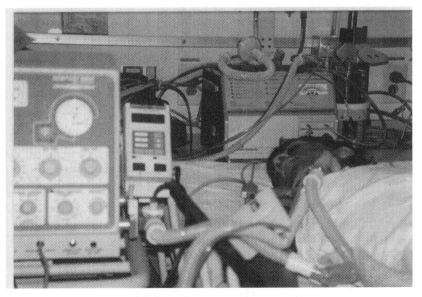

12. At sixteen after the trache was reinserted.

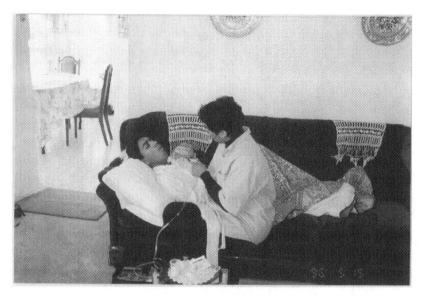

13. Being deep-suctioned by mom.

14. My high school prom in 1999.

15. Sightseeing in Tobago.

16. With Auntie Ishra who bought me for twenty-five cents.

17. My twenty-first birthday, with two nurses:
(left) Ruth Scholz and Pam Laverty.

18. With Aunt Yasmin at my twenty-first birthday celebration.

19. With Dr. Pitt-Miller at the Faculty of Medicine in Trinidad.

20. In Trinidad with Mrs. Bratt (left) and Dr. Bratt.

21. From left: Paul, Azeem, Jim Carr and Jed DeCory.
Paul was the first recipient of the Azeem Kayum Scholarship Award.

22. With my cousin Nadeem in Tobago.

23. With Dr. John Edmonds after my college convocation.

24. Speaking at my book launching in Trinidad in 2004.

25. Addressing a corporate gathering.

Chapter 12
Locked Out in Tennessee

The blaring sounds of the sirens had people curious. The vehicles pulled into the parking lot of the fast-food restaurant. Mom was sweating in the midday sun. My dad, on the other hand, was flustered. This was one time when he was not the calm individual he usually is. Everyone in the restaurant was looking to see why the ambulance and fire trucks were called. There was no accident. No fire. No excitement. Little did they know I was the cause.

We were travelling along Interstate 75 on the way to Florida. Those drives are usually quite relaxing for me and I really look forward to eating at the various fast food joints. We all started feeling hungry, so my dad pulled into the next fast-food outlet. Our stops were usually short since our goal was to get to our destination as quickly as possible and begin our holiday. As we got out of the van and headed to the restaurant, my mom turned to me.

"Did you suction?"

"No, I don't need to," I quickly replied.

"You should before you begin eating," she insisted.

"But I don't need to," I repeated, feeling pressured.

"Oh, no!" my dad exclaimed.

We all looked at him. He was tapping his pants pocket.

"Don't tell me," my mom said.

"Yes, I did. I locked the keys in the van." He sounded angry with himself.

He headed back to the vehicle, and sure enough, the key was still in the ignition.

"Don't worry, I have my keys." Mom sounded relieved, but that soon changed because she realized the she had left her handbag in the van.

Hell! I thought. My suction kit was in the van. I felt the instant pressure. Mucus was starting to build up in my lungs. A few seconds made such a difference. Stress and anxiety do that to me.

Dad looked around the van to see if any door was opened. They were all locked. He checked the windows. There was only a tiny space on the passenger's side window through which no hand could pass. There was no way to get in, so he quickly dialed 911. He informed the operator about the situation, stressing that medical equipment was locked in the vehicle. Within minutes, a fire truck arrived. Like my dad, the fire fighters checked to see if they could find a way to get in, but they could not.

Then Dad said, "Oh, our daughter has long, skinny arms so she could try." My sister, totally embarrassed, tried but did not succeed. The firemen used a piece of wire to get through the tiny crease but were still unable to get to the lock.

During that time, I was becoming more uncomfortable. My nose had started to flare out, a sign that respiratory problems could follow. My parents would have to take me to the nearest hospital if the situation became worse. My dad was trying to help the firemen, while at the same time keeping tabs on my condition. Everyone in the restaurant was aware that it was a serious case. Just seeing the firemen struggling to open the door was enough to let the onlookers know something was wrong. And yes, our van was parked in the area reserved for people with special needs.

At one point, the firemen thought of breaking the window. Luckily, that did not happen. It would have been a bad start to the holiday. In a last-ditch effort, with the wire in his hand, one of the firemen hooked the lock and pulled it really hard. Bingo! The door was opened. Quickly, Mom rushed me to the van so I could be suctioned. So many people were looking at me. Being a self-conscious young boy, who had just turned fifteen, I did not have time to be embarrassed. I gagged and gagged. I am pretty sure some onlookers felt sorry for me. So much mucus came out of my lungs. It was unbelievable! But I felt relieved and was able to breathe easily once again.

Coughing was not automatic for me at that time. People cough to remove mucus, but I needed a suction kit to do that for me. The muscles in my neck were not developed to perform something so natural. When I had my trache removed later on, I was given a machine called a Coffalator, which was used to trigger coughs. After using it for a month or two, I was able to cough on my own. However, I still experience difficulties when I have a severe infection.

The drama came to an end. We thanked the firemen for being so helpful. They were more at ease after I suctioned myself. They wished us well for the remainder of our trip and headed back to their fire station.

What an experience! It is one I will never forget. I sensed the anxiety of my parents. How badly they must have felt. We did not expect to spend two hours at the stop, but there was no other alternative. We ate quickly and continued our journey. It was not the way we expected things to go. Being locked out in Tennessee was no fun.

Chapter 13
My First Leather Jacket

Scotiabank gave me my first chance in the working environment, a chance to see what the real world was all about. For that, I will always be grateful.

In my mom's book, she mentioned the accommodation and flexibility made by Scotiabank, both to her when she was working there, and to Dad during the most crucial periods of my life. He has been working at Scotiabank since 1973.

In the summer of 1996, when I was seventeen years old, my parents, believing that I should live as normal a life as possible, approached me about volunteering for the summer at Scotiabank's Toronto Call Centre. *Why Scotiabank and not World Wrestling Entertainment's (WWE) head office in Toronto?* I wondered. Wrestling has always been my passion. Quickly, I realized why. My medical condition prevented me from doing the kind of volunteer work I would have been excited about—wrestling commentary! At that time, I still needed suctioning on a regular basis. Would the WWE want to take the risk? How would other staff members feel? At least at Scotiabank, Dad would be around in the event of a medical emergency. Many of his colleagues at work knew about me, and hopefully they would be more sensitive to my medical condition, my limitations and my fears of working for the first time.

Once I agreed, Dad told me he was not sure whether Scotiabank would accept me as a volunteer because in his many years at the bank, he had never seen any summer students volunteering, especially those with special needs. The bank hired summer students, but they had to be at least eighteen years of age. Again, I would be breaking new ground because I was still a year shy of my eighteenth birthday. At that time, Bob Stark was the senior vice-president of Scotiabank's Call Centre. He was a real sharp, young individual and one of the main speakers at Mom's book launching in 1995. That was when I first met him and other Scotiabank employees. Bob's presentation was very impressive and he really had a great impact on the audience.

Bob would be the person to approach about the volunteer position, and if he agreed, the Bank's Human Resources Department would also have to give its consent. However, Dad first met with the senior manager of his department, David Collins, to see if he would be willing to accept me as a volunteer. They discussed a few duties I could perform. David was agreeable and suggested my father discuss the unusual request with Bob. Again, there was no problem.

But as we expected, Bob mentioned that the bank's Human Resources Department would have to approve such an arrangement. Another meeting was scheduled with the Human Resources manager, Ann Ferguson, to discuss this matter. Ann stressed the uniqueness of the request and said she would have to speak to her management team. A few days later, she responded favourably. The Human Resources Department felt the request was reasonable and did not go against any of the bank's policies. She suggested the request to volunteer be formally documented.

The entire approval process took about one week. No one thought it would be that easy. Our family had grown accustomed to facing obstacles and having to fight hard to overcome them.

So there I was in the summer of 1996, going to work for the first time in my life, volunteering three days a week. It was decided before I started that I would assist in processing the questionnaires and customer surveys which customers returned to the bank.

About eight people worked in the department. They were all very kind to me. They showed care and concern and went out of their way to make me feel comfortable. They wanted me to succeed. They wanted my first experience to be pleasant. My boss, Anita Murray, was patient and understanding.

Happily, my desk was not close to my dad's office, and I believe he wanted it that way so I could feel a bit of independence. After all, throughout my life I have always had medical supervision, and it was a big relief not having a nurse around me.

The only times I interacted with my father were when I required suctioning and during lunch. For the suctioning, I would go to his office and extract the mucus from my lungs. Knowing how much I loved to eat out, he took me almost every day to one of the nearby fast-food joints.

Working was fun but very tiring. I worked from 8:30 AM to 4:30 PM. It was a great experience for me, though at times I was frustrated because I could not do specific tasks correctly. It was during the time I was working there I received the Anne and Ed Mirvish Award (which I write about in chapter 15). My coworkers read the article in the *Toronto Star*. They were all proud of me. They felt because of what I had accomplished in my life, it was only fitting that I receive such a prestigious award.

The following year, my parents asked me if I wanted to volunteer again at Scotiabank. Based on my enjoyable experience the previous year, I willingly agreed.

To broaden my working experience, Dad approached a senior management officer in another department. He had worked for this man for many years. His name was Owen Marsh. I met Owen as a child during one of my visits to the bank, and for some reason I always remembered him. He left a good impression on me.

Fortunately, the approval process was not necessary. Also, I was now eighteen years old. I believe that Owen discussed my situation with the Vice-President, Mike Hayes, to whom he reported. I remember being introduced to Mike the year before when I volunteered there.

Once Mike and Owen agreed to hire me, it was just a matter of finding a proper placement. Owen could not find a suitable job for me in his area and approached one of his peers in another department within the Call Centre. This man's name was Doug Dees, the assistant general manager of the National Retail Credit Centre of Scotiabank. Together, they decided that they would try to place me for the summer in one of their vacant positions.

However, this time around the arrangement would be different. I had to apply for a vacant position, which meant they would be paying me. I was excited about the thought of earning my own money for the first time in my life. I had my eyes on a classy leather jacket, and I figured it would be my big chance to own that.

One of my favorite things is a motorcycle. Although I know I will never ride one, I always picture myself wearing a stylish jacket while riding a motorcycle. Even if I were normal, my parents would not have given me permission to get myself a bike. So I settled for the leather jacket instead. (My dad recently told me that Doug also rides a motorbike as a hobby. Maybe I should reconnect with him and see if he would take me for a ride, but then my parents might "disconnect" me!)

With some guidance from dad, I applied for the position of credit clerk. A few days later, I was called in for two interviews. I was advised I had to be interviewed for the position by the Call

Centre Human Resources Department and by one of the management officers of the department.

What would they ask me? Why did I have to go through this process? But I wanted the leather jacket badly, so I told myself I had to perform well in the interviews.

My father was not very helpful as I began preparing for the interviews the weekend before. He told me he had not hired anyone in years, and from what he found out, the process had changed. Oh, no! However, he gave me some idea of the questions he would ask if he had to hire someone. I jotted those down, along with my answers and then Mom and I started role playing. That exercise gave me some confidence and I tried to memorize most of the answers.

My parents warned me that there was no guarantee I would land the job and a lot would depend on how I did at the interviews. The pressure was on and they were making it more difficult for me. But, looking back, I realize that they were preparing me for the real world, and they did not want me to build up my hopes too much.

The day of the interviews finally came. I have had interviews with radio personnel and television networks and I looked forward to them. I was nervous for those interviews; but for the job interviews I was ten times as nervous. Butterflies were in my stomach. I had the jitters. The fear was real. I have always had problems vocalizing when I am nervous, so I had every reason to be afraid. The leather jacket was finally within reach and I could not let the chance slip by.

Once the interviews began, I settled down. But I stuttered and during the interviews the stuttering became worse. Processing the questions asked and trying to answer them without sounding stupid were thoughts that popped into my head. I wanted to do well in the interview for myself. I also did not want to embarrass my father. What stress! What pressure! In my opinion, I could have done better. I used too much effort to get my voice and words out. I think the officers who interviewed me realized my disabilities were preventing me from responding quickly and they were very patient. Thank God!

Surprisingly, I got the job. It required me to do a series of different tasks, like sorting and distributing mail, checking applications to make sure the necessary information was given and at times returning those applications to the branches for additional information.

I quickly got the hang of things. But I was not performing like my co-workers. I was much slower. Using a staple remover was difficult for me. My poor fine-motor skills were evident. Even using a letter opener was tough. My mom made me repeat those tasks at home on evenings after work. Imagine having to learn how to use a staple remover! As for the letter opener, that was torture. I had major problems getting the tip of the opener into the small opening of the envelope. But holding the envelope with one hand and sliding the letter opener along the seam of the envelope was even more difficult. It took me a few days to master the skill. Despite that, I concentrated on getting the work done accurately. After two weeks, I was given my first pay check. I worked for it. And yes, it felt great to receive it!

I spent the remaining six weeks working hard and doing my best. The management and staff treated me like one of the team. They were patient and reached out to me. The summer came to an end. All I had on my mind was the leather jacket. My parents made this event even more special by taking me to Niagara Falls for dinner. Then we all went shopping for my leather jacket.

As I entered the store that specialized in leather coats, I was on a high because I could not believe I was so close to making a dream come true. (Or maybe I was on a high because of the smell of leather!) There were too many jackets to choose from. I knew what I wanted. Something simple, one like a biker wears. Short, with studs and a zipped front. I flipped through the hangers. I took my time and I did not feel any pressure from my parents to hurry. They knew how much this purchase meant to me.

I chose about four from the rack. Just holding the hangers in my hand was like a dream. When my arm slipped through the second sleeve, I could not control myself. I admired what I saw in the mirror. Each one looked fantastic. But I had to choose one. How could I? I liked them all. I spent a long time trying them on over and over again. Since I always liked the biker jackets, I felt myself leaning toward the one closest to that style. My decision was made. I took out my wallet and checked my notes. I was spending my hard-earned money to purchase something I wanted. What fun it was!

I have fond memories of working at Scotiabank. I am convinced the people who interviewed me looked beyond my disabilities. I think they zeroed in on my abilities instead.

Everyone should focus on a person's strengths, even if they are few. At a small thanksgiving function held after my graduation from college, Mom, in her address to the audience, encouraged employers to give people with disabilities a chance.

Mom and I attended the Abilities 2003 Job Fair, where David Onley, from City Pulse TV, gave the keynote address. Like my mother, he pointed out that "employers have the capability of transforming lives." He told his listeners they, too, can touch the life of someone with a disability and "make a difference."

Scotiabank gave me the opportunity—my first paying job! I bought my first leather jacket, which I still have and wear to this day. I have since purchased my second jacket, one that is a little more conservative. But the first jacket will always be my favourite.

Chapter 14

High School Prom

For most of my life, I have proven people wrong. It was not something I set out to do. It just happened that way. Medically, I did not have much control. My life was in the hands of God, doctors, nurses, bureaucrats, social workers, therapists, teachers and of course, my parents. While my own courage played a big role in my survival, medical decisions were made for me in my early life. I would have done nothing differently.

With my education, I had more control. I had to work very hard. High school was tough. Assignments. Projects. Deadlines. I received a lot of support and assistance from my parents, especially my mom. She keeps reminding me and other people that I am the one who made it all happen. "He showed interest. He was determined," she says. I like that. *I* did it. *I* was the one who worked hard. *I* was the one who stayed up late. *I* went the extra mile to complete everything I needed to. And she gave me credit for my efforts.

If I did not have the drive and will to succeed, the ability to shut out the negatives, especially the feeling of isolation, I would have flunked. As always, I felt God was pulling for me. I talked to him. He made me go on. He picked me up many times when I was ready to give in. There were many days when I felt the struggle was too much. I felt sorry for myself. Nobody could understand the chaos I endured. That remains between God and me.

So, on the one hand, I knew the doctors did not expect me to live, and yet here I am writing about my experiences so many years later. On the other hand, I told myself that since I survived so long, I might live for another few decades. Then what? I had to have some form of education. There were many near-death experiences, but I had to do my best to succeed for my future well-being and I did.

My parents coached and counselled me. "Keep focused," they would say. Those familiar words have become one of my mottos. People felt they were words of pressure, but those words pulled me back in line. My parents live them every day. They keep reminding me that I am capable of doing anything I set out to do. They do not expect it to be done overnight, but they tell me, "If you set realistic goals and work to achieve them, you will succeed."

Someone who is a qualified counsellor does not always make a good one. Very often that person does not live the experience. While my parents are not counsellors by profession, in my mind they are. My dad has a calm way about him. When he speaks, he can put anyone at ease. He offers great advice, always being very fair and outspoken, which gets him into trouble sometimes. His aura always has a soothing effect on me. He is blessed with a great sense of humour and tons of patience. However, do not ever get him upset. He shoots from the hip and never minces his words. Whenever he counsels others, he is very upfront and straightforward.

My mom is very realistic and practical. She tells other parents that results will come with work. She reminds them about "patience and reward." I know she talks from her experiences, and her advice comes from her heart. If my parents feel sorry for me, they don't show it. They always discourage self-pity and remind me about working hard in order to achieve.

With a high school diploma, I thought I was through studying. Even though I applied to colleges, I was not thinking far ahead. I felt I had accomplished a lot. It may not sound like a big deal to many people, but what an achievement for me!

Not only did I finish high school in grade twelve, but I finished grade thirteen, also known as Ontario Academic Credits (OAC). I didn't do the bare minimum of six subjects, but finished seven. My friends gave me a thumbs up. My parents and sister were very pleased with my success. Close friends and family joined in my happiness.

But a more important occasion was on my mind—prom. I was not going to miss prom for anything. There was a lot of talk about prom: clothes, hairstyles, limos and who was taking whom. A buzz was in the air and I was part of that.

I had to shop for my tuxedo. Shopping has always been difficult for me. When my movements slowly came back after my birth injury, my growth was affected. My right side is more developed than the left. So finding suitable clothing has always been a challenge. After days of looking around, I made my choices. The tux would have to be altered.

My mom detests sewing. Fixing a button on a shirt is a chore. She could have left the tux at the store to be altered, but it would mean spending more money; and since she always thinks about cutting costs, she chose to frustrate herself and complete the required adjustments. The shoes, which we bought, also needed some work before fitting properly, because my left foot is shorter and narrower than the right one.

Everything was ready, and I waited for the big day. The time was going by too slowly. A few days before the prom, my mom ironed my shirt, steam pressed the hem of my pants and hung up everything. I admired the purchases and pictured myself in the tuxedo. "A hunk of chunk," as my dad always said. I smiled at the thought. I was truly happy.

The excitement about the prom was real. Some of my friends were talking about their dates. Panic hit me. I could not ask a girl. I was afraid of being turned down. Who would want to go with me? I had many female friends, but I did not think anyone would wish to accompany me. While I have a great deal of confidence, I needed some more to get over that hump.

As I was with my friends one day, one of them, Anant, noticed my anxiety and talked to me. He has been my friend since public school, so he knew I was disturbed.

"Hey, man, you're quiet."

"Yeah, just listening."

"Sure you're okay?"

Most times when I am quiet, my friends think I am getting sick. Little did they know what was going on in my mind.

"Yep. Listening to you people talk about your dates."

"Oh, so you are okay. Well, tell us, man, who are you taking?"

"That's my worry. I have no one."

My friends, realizing I was a little embarrassed, pepped me up.

"Hey, don't let a woman get you down. Some guys aren't taking dates."

"Really? That's cool! There's hope for me."

"I don't want a woman to hold me back. I want to have a good time with my buddies," one friend said.

"I agree," echoed another. "When you take a woman, you have to make sure she's okay."

"And then you can't leave her and go dance with your friends. She might get an attitude," someone else added.

The conversation was going the way I hoped. Not everyone was taking a date. I would not be the odd ball. I would not be isolated and lonely at such an important occasion.

"So, A.K., don't make a woman keep you back. Four of us in the group will be hanging loose that night. Pretty sure others will also."

"Thanks, man. I feel better." A huge weight was off my shoulders.

As I was dressing for the prom, the phone rang. My aunts and grandparents in Trinidad were calling to share my excitement. My aunts would have gone shopping with me if they were living in Canada. They would have jumped at the opportunity to tag along when my parents took me to the prom. They would have been at my home fussing over me. In fact, Yassy, my mom's sister, spoke to me before I left, saying, "All those girls will sure check you out tonight."

"Be quiet, please," I answered, but she continued joyfully.

"I know they will, but which one will you be taking?"

My responses only encouraged her to continue. So I decided not to answer her. She poked and pried, hoping to get it out of me, but I did not give her any information. My other aunt, Shereen (Teen, to us), came on the line and continued the fussing. Grandpa Baksh and Grammies (my maternal grandparents) were excited. I heard it in their voices. My aunts and grandparents shared with me their pride and joy. They truly know how to make me feel special. That simple phone call meant a lot to me. That is one of the little things that keeps me going. I really wished they could have been with me on that special day.

It was a long drive, about forty-five minutes, to the venue. I was bubbling over with excitement. My parents always made sure I looked good. They could not afford the brand-name items, so I dressed in less expensive clothes. Brand-name clothing does not make one look any better anyway. I do not always have to wear brand names to boost my self-esteem.

When we arrived at the hall, a few students were already there. My friends were not there yet, so I stayed in the van with my parents. My mom was "oohing" and "ahhing" as the limos started arriving. They came in all shapes, sizes and colours. My mom had to comment on every dress: which one was too grown up, which one was too short, which one was perfect. She carried on and on. She had comments about the guys as well. She really liked the way one of my classmates, Ben, looked with his top hat. I am sure my dad also liked what he saw of the ladies!

The hall was decorated simply—just a few bunches of balloons. My mom, who is also a certified balloon decorator, could have done a better job. And knowing it was my prom, she would have gone all out. As I headed to my assigned table, I glanced around. The hall was becoming filled. And what a sight! Everyone looked really special. The teachers who were there were all cool. They had to make sure the students behaved themselves. Shortly after we settled, dinner was served. The meal was one of the worst I have ever tasted—a small piece of chicken, potatoes, and veggies. Small amounts for big bucks! However, the meal was not really important that night.

A funny video was shown during dinner. There were clips of students in awkward and funny situations at school. Memories came back so clearly. After everyone had dessert, the dancing began. Even those who did not have dates were on the floor. Although I have a problem with my balance, I partied away and had fun. I might have looked odd, but it was my night and nobody was going to stop me from having a great time!

By midnight, the celebrations came to a memorable end. Some of us parted with hugs and kisses, knowing we might never see each other again. Some headed to other parties. My group of friends went to a campsite for the weekend. I wanted to go in the worst way. I begged my parents to let me go, but they refused.

Even my aunts in Trinidad begged for me. They did it to make me feel good, but I knew they realized it would be too dangerous. I would have to go with my respirator. My parents were not prepared to take the chance, even though I stated that I believed I could go a couple nights without the machine. As much as I begged and pleaded, I also knew the dangers involved. I thought I would sway them somehow, but I didn't.

My dream night, which left me with so many wonderful memories, ended. I was on a high for many days after.

All my hard work in high school had paid off. I was successful in yet another phase of my life. Some of my teachers and the consultant at the Board of Education had not recommended a normal high school education for me. But, through lots of dedication, perseverance, hard work, and support from my parents, I did it—and in a regular school! I defied those who wanted me to attend a special school, where I would learn a special trade or be "at the top of the class." Never was I at the top of the class at Markville Secondary, but what a joy it was for me to say I finished high school, integrated with normal teens, and even completed seven OAC courses. The only concession my teachers made for me was giving me extra time during exams.

If my parents had listened to the educators' recommendations, I cannot imagine what would have happened to me. Those of us with disabilities have potential but are stifled by those in authority. Look at what I have accomplished! I graduated from high school. Not every challenged individual will succeed, but then, neither will every normal child.

Teachers should observe children with special needs. Look for good work habits, parental support, dedication and the will to achieve. Then, and only then, should the teacher recommend. I am not a teacher and do not intend to become one, but I have listened to my parents' discussions on placement and I learned what works. Hopefully, some teachers will look at challenged students in a different light, because mentally challenged children are capable. They can succeed if they are given the chance!

I was given a chance and am very grateful to my parents for fighting for me. I am also thankful to those who stood up for me at school and who included me in the fun and merriment on prom night.

Chapter 15

A Major Recognition

One morning, Mom received a surprising phone call from a man named Russell Lazar. He introduced himself as the general manager of "Honest Ed's" (a store in Toronto once owned by the late Ed Mirvish) and informed her that Mirvish Enterprises gives out an annual award to a young person in the community who demonstrates courage and determination, and I was selected to be that year's recipient. Mr. Lazar also stated the recognition came with a $3,000 cash award, which would be presented at the Ed Mirvish annual birthday celebration on Sunday, July 21, 1996.

My mom asked the Mr. Lazar how they heard about me. He told her they were impressed with my grit and determination, as reported in the *Toronto Star*, on Friday, March 1, 1996. And they could not think of a more suitable candidate for the award. That article, with the headline "The Boy Who Wouldn't Die," was featured three months after Mom published her book, *For a Breath of Life*.

Here is what the *Toronto Star* reporter, Robin Harvey, wrote:

The Boy Who Wouldn't Die
By Robin Harvey, Staff Reporter

Some people thought Azeem Kayum was crazy when he decided to go out for track last year and enter the 100-metre dash.

"I came in last, but I was still in the race," the 16-year-old Grade 9 student says, flashing a heart-melting grin.

It sums up the Stouffville teen's attitude so well, it should be emblazoned on his T-shirt. Doctors had initially said Azeem, who was born paralyzed from the neck down after a birth injury caused severe respiratory and spinal cord damage, would never walk or talk.

At one point early in his life, his parents were advised to pull the plug and they had planned his funeral.

But, Azeem has beaten all the odds and turned 16 in December.

Though he has many medical problems and some degree of learning disability, he remains a fighter who has developed a razor-sharp wit balanced by a winning charm.

"You have to do what's opposite of what they expect you to do. If that's nothing—do something. Don't give in."

Azeem spent his first year in the Intensive Care Unit at the Hospital for Sick Children. At age 2 1/2, he suffered two cardiac arrests in 10 days and was in a coma for nearly two weeks. In the end, he had to have a surgical opening put in his throat so he can breathe at night with a ventilator.

As a result, everywhere he goes, he must take a portable suctioning device to clear his tracheostomy opening—on a good day, as often as six times a day, on a bad one, more than a dozen.

In the last few years, he has undergone surgery on his legs because they were not developing properly due to his partial paralysis. He can't do anything strenuous, and even a mild cold can be life-threatening as any type of infection hampers his already delicate and undependable breathing.

But, he says he never let it get him down.

"There was that time I almost died," he says of a particularly serious bout of breathing trouble, when he tried, unsuccessfully, to wean himself off nighttime ventilation. "But, I made it."

Azeem's special education teacher, Beverly Carson, who is now in charge of monitoring his progress at Markville Secondary School, says he's "simply amazing."

"I have never encountered such a diligent, dedicated, wonderful young man," she says. "He is a wonderful role model for all the other students. His positive attitude wears off on everyone. I feel honored to work with him."

Asked what his goals for the future are, he points to the dime-sized hole through which he breathes at night and suctions his throat during the day.

"Getting this thing removed." If he didn't have the trache, and could breathe better on his own at night, Azeem says he'd be more independent. Now he has to have a nurse or parent with him wherever he goes.

"It's tough on the social life."

"People ask me in school about the trache. They don't understand. Someone asked me if it was a decoration. I wish," he says as he rolls his eyes.

He was somewhat embarrassed that his mother had to go to his high school earlier this year to explain the suctioning device and his medical problems to the students. "Now they've gotten used to it because my mom went and talked to the kids. They wouldn't accept me."

That's part of the reason he's so supportive of his mother's latest project—a self-published book that outlines his and his family's struggles.

"The book is going to let people know what is going on. I'm just a guy."

Despite his obvious close ties to his mother, Azeem unceremoniously shoos her out of the room to conduct this interview alone.

Like most teens, Azeem is walking the line between dependence and independence—a journey made tougher by his physical limitations. Still, he went out for a public speaking contest in Grade 6, and made it to the finals, speaking on the topic "The Brain and Me."

His father, Faizal, who works as a senior consultant at a bank, his younger sister, Lisaan, and his mother watched a videotape of the contest, fearing if they went in person, Azeem would be too nervous.

In his speech, he told about how the brain functions and how his had been damaged with the result that he could not automatically breathe when he is sleeping. He summed up with, "Wear helmets when you ride your bikes. Do what you can to protect your brain. Don't take it for granted. I know how tough it is when your brain does not work well. Trust me, it can be very frustrating at times."

Today, Azeem says he'd like to eventually end up as a wrestling commentator.

"They have most of it memorized, so my reading shouldn't be a problem."

He's been hooked on the WWF since age five. His hero is Shawn Michaels, and he spends hours reading wrestling magazines. He dreams of being hooked up to the Internet so he can access the wrestling Web sites.

Beyond that, Azeem says other important things in his life are girls, music, and friends. His family has their house up for sale so he can be close to his high school in Markham. The family lives in Stouffville, and Azeem is driven to school every day in their van.

That way, he'd be able to go out with his friends more often, like when he went to see *Mortal Kombat* in the summer.

Food is also big on his list of likes. He likes to eat two Whoppers when he goes to Burger King. He also likes to help his mother cook.

Azeem has met with other young kids living with a trache. He gives everybody the same advice he gives himself.

"Just never give up. Live life one day at a time," he says. "I try to procure a lot of self-esteem. You have to build your confidence."

Mr. Lazar also told Mom a formal letter about the award would be mailed to us.

Mom was skeptical and didn't tell me about the phone call. She immediately called my dad, who also had some reservations. They decided they would wait on the letter and then tell me about the award.

The letter arrived a few days later. My parents showed it to me and I could not believe it, especially the part about the $3,000 award. I was seventeen, and for me that was a lot of money. My parents indicated to me that the purpose of the $3,000 award was for me to use toward my college or university education. I did not mind because I was beginning to understand the financial struggles my parents were experiencing, trying to survive mainly on my dad's income. My mom was forced to give up her career to care for me and worked on and off around my needs and schedule.

I read the letter over and over. Here is what it said:

Dear Azeem,

We are pleased to inform you that you will be this year's recipient of the "Anne and Ed Mirvish Achievement Award for Young People."

A short presentation will take place on Sunday, July 21st at approximately 12 noon. We hope you will be able to join us for the ceremonies.

We ask that you not make this notice public as we will be making a news release sometime in July.

We will be in contact with you prior to July 21st.

Keep up the good work and once again congratulations.

Sincerely,
Russell Lazar
General Manager
Ed Mirvish Enterprises

Chapter 16

The Anne and
Ed Mirvish Award

Despite my disabilities, I always like to dress well and look good. When my aunts in Trinidad, especially Yassy and Teen, spent their summers with us, they would not only bring a lot of clothes sent from Trinidad by their other sisters and cousins, but they purchased so much more for me while they were in Canada. I wanted to dress well when presented with my award.

The week before Honest Ed's birthday bash, Ed Mirvish Enterprises sent the following press release to the *Toronto Star* about my award:

> Teen who's battled handicap wins award for achievement
> $3,000 cash gift goes to boy born paralyzed from neck down.
> By Kathleen Goldhar
>
> Almost from the day he was born, Azeem Kayum was determined never to give up.
> The 16-year-old Stouffville teen, who has won the Anne and Ed Mirvish Achievement Award for Young People, was born paralyzed from the neck down after

a birth injury caused severe respiratory and spinal cord damage.

Doctors didn't expect him to live. His parents were advised to pull the plug and had even planned a funeral.

But with therapy, and a lot of help from his family, Azeem started walking just after he turned 2.

"It's an honor" to receive this award, said Azeem, who feels "just like a normal human being," despite his health problems.

Azeem will be presented with the award, which was instituted three years ago to recognize young people for outstanding achievement, and a $3,000 cash gift on July 21 at Ed Mirvish's birthday party celebrations.

The decision to select Azeem was not because he is physically disabled, say the Mirvishes. The "diligent, dedicated young man" is a role model to his fellow students at Markville Secondary School, they said.

The award was "one of the best things that could have happened to him," said his mother, Laila.

At 2 1/2, Azeem suffered two cardiac arrests in ten days. Afterwards, he had trouble breathing at nights and had to have a surgical opening in his throat.

In April, Azeem had the "trache," the tube in his throat removed—something he had been dreaming about for years. Unfortunately, he could only go two weeks without it.

On Mother's Day, Azeem told his family he was having too much trouble breathing without the trache and thought he needed it back in.

"He felt defeated," said his mother, who quit her job when Azeem was born to work full-time on his recovery.

The day Azeem came home from the hospital was the day he received the message that he won the award.

"It did a lot for his self-confidence," said his mother, who feels the strength she found to continually encourage her son to never give up "is more powerful than we can put into words."

Sunday July 21, 1996, arrived. It was Ed Mirvish's big birthday bash. We had never gone to any of the previous celebrations and we did not know what to expect. My parents made sure I wore a brand-new suit for the all-day gala. It was a pleasant, sunny summer day. The presentation ceremonies were set for noon.

My mom, dad, paternal grandparents, my high school special education teacher, Beverly Carson, her friend, Violet Mintschef, and some of our close friends agreed to attend the party. My sister was spending the summer in Trinidad. My parents told me I might be expected to thank Anne and Ed Mirvish for the award, so I should be prepared. A few days before the event, I spent some time putting together my acceptance speech.

We arrived at "Honest Ed's" around eleven in the morning and were immediately escorted into the dining room. We were then introduced to Anne and Ed Mirvish and to the general manager, Russell Lazar. They congratulated me and made us all feel quite comfortable. Anne congratulated Mom on the book she had written and praised my parents for their hard work.

I expected to see a more excitable "Honest Ed," the one we were used to seeing on television commercials. He was statesman-like, professional, warm, and very friendly. His wife was much more talkative. She was dressed like royalty and chatted with us in greater detail. I assume "Honest Ed" was more focused on the formalities and the speech he had to deliver.

A little later, we stepped outside and were shocked to see how quickly the crowd was gathering. We were then escorted to the VIP sitting area just in front of the stage, where the programme was about to begin.

As I looked at the crowd of about ten thousand, I became a bit nervous. It was close to noon and the sunshine was beginning to take its toll on me. It was at the peak of the summer and I was all dressed up in my new suit, shirt and tie.

I felt nervous and anxious. As a result, I started to accumulate mucus in my trachea and required suctioning. I wanted to clear my lungs before the programme started. My dad took me out of the VIP area and we went back to a more private place, where I did what was necessary.

A few minutes after noon, Mr. Lazar invited me to come up on the stage. My dad helped me up the steps, where I joined the Mirvishes and several dignitaries, including a few local politicians. My parents and our guests were at ground level, just as excited and nervous as I was.

If they had seen what I saw, they would have passed out. It was something out of this world. I had never seen so many people together in my life. The stage was built at the head of Markham and Bloor streets in downtown Toronto. As I looked down Markham Street, I only saw people, people, and more people. It was truly amazing. I started to sweat more in the heat. My legs started to buckle. How could I stand up and deliver a speech to so many people? I am sure there were more than twenty thousand people in attendance.

I began to think. *Should I just accept the award, say thank you and wait out the rest of the formalities, or should I stick to my plan?*

Since I was in public school, I was gifted with the courage and strength to speak in public. I had spoken at family gatherings and at book-launching events in Toronto, Maryland and Trinidad, after mom's book was published. I even made a few speeches in some of the mosques in Toronto and at my family's thanksgiving services. In those gatherings, the audiences ranged anywhere from fifty to five hundred. I was always nervous prior to the speeches, but once I started to speak, the anxiety disappeared.

I debated quietly within myself. My acceptance speech was only about one minute long and it was somewhat inspirational. I looked at my teacher, Bev Carson. She had helped me a lot in high school and I could not let her down. I looked at my parents and grandparents and I knew they were proud of me and would feel much prouder if I proceeded with the speech. I could not let them down either. I said a silent prayer and decided to stick to the original plan.

After a brief introduction by Mr. Lazar, I was presented with the award by Anne and Ed Mirvish. Then, I delivered my speech:

Master of Ceremonies, Mr. and Mrs. Mirvish, Distinguished Guests, Ladies and Gentlemen,

I would like to thank Ed Mirvish Enterprises for this special Achievement Award in honor of Mr. Mirvish's birthday. My parents told me that Mr. Mirvish and I share at least one common trait. We have defied all the odds. I have survived.

When I was born, I did not breathe or move for several days and the doctors did not expect me to live beyond a few days, a few weeks, or even a few months. Although I am still challenged and still sleep with a respirator every night, I continue to do better than anyone expected—just like Mr. Mirvish. I would like to publicly thank all those who helped me to do this. First, Almighty God, all the doctors and nurses at The Hospital for Sick Children in Toronto, my family doctor, Dr. Drutz, my relatives, my teachers, my friends, and especially my parents.

My mom has written a book on my life. In the book, *For a Breath of Life*, she wrote that one of my dreams is to become a wrestling commentator. Mr. Mirvish, I am sure this award will help me realize that dream.

My sincere thanks again to Ed Mirvish Enterprises, and a very happy birthday to you, Mr. Mirvish.

That was my moment of glory. I came, I saw and I delivered! Once the opening ceremonies were completed, I was interviewed by the radio and television networks that were there to cover the event. Many people came up afterwards and congratulated me both for my bravery and for my strong willpower. I did it. I spoke to one of the largest crowds I had ever seen!

We stayed at the party for a couple of hours, listening to the bands and entertainers who were invited to share their talents at "Honest Ed's" grand birthday celebration.

That moment of happiness lasted for several weeks and months. Even now, as I look back on that day, I feel very proud of myself and the beautiful memories will remain with me until I die.

The inscription on the plaque I received reads:

Anne & Ed Mirvish Achievement Award For Young People
Presented to Azeem Kayum
For Outstanding Achievement

In that despite many life-threatening setbacks during his young years, Azeem is a role model whose courage, resilience, dedication and determination have inspired us all.

We congratulate you, Azeem.

July 21, 1996

I am sure Anne and Ed Mirvish would be very pleased to know the award money was used to pay for part of my tuition fees at Seneca College.

Mr. Mirvish and his team looked at my accomplishments and other positive qualities when they were selecting the recipient of the award. They recognized me for my abilities. I am sure they will continue to make a difference in the lives of many people. They made a difference in mine!

Chapter 17
Home Away from Home

Six operations from ages two to fourteen, several bouts of pneumonia, respirator failures, brain scans, sleep studies, cardiograms—the list is endless. The hospital and medical procedures became familiar to me. At a very young age, I was leading the way to the different clinics. No child likes the environment of a clinic or hospital, yet I was comfortable. I felt I belonged there. I felt safe and secure. The entire first year of my life was spent at The Hospital for Sick Children in Toronto, but I cannot relive a single memory. It was my first home.

My parents speak so well of the care and attention given to me by the doctors and nurses at the hospital. Pictures tell a thousand tales. There are so many photographs of me when I lived there. The nurses and doctors always rooted for me and formed some kind of special bond with me. I was a permanent resident. There was no paperwork or documentation stating I was one, but where else could I have gone? Yes, I was assigned a little corner of a big room, and my parents were given permission to take in my clothes and toys to make my surroundings feel like home. I did not have to pay a rent to live in the room—at least, my parents did not. My care was very expensive and paid for by Ontario's Health Insurance Plan (OHIP) and Dad's Medical Insurance Plan with Scotiabank.

I often hear my parents talk about their relationship with the medical staff. From what I gather, Mom and Dad formed a strong bond with them. I saw a few of the doctors and nurses when Mom launched her book, as well as on my eighteenth and twenty-first birthday celebrations.

Dr. Karen Pape was the doctor on duty when I was admitted. I am pretty sure I must have tested her capabilities as a young doctor and scared the hell out of her. She did a fantastic job, based on what I heard and read in Mom's book. Having a rare condition and a doctor who was relatively new in her post, I must have challenged her. She monitored me until I was about fourteen. I have very pleasant memories of her; she was always friendly, cheerful, and humorous.

Then came Dr. John Edmonds. He is still my buddy. I still e-mail him occasionally just to keep in touch, and he responds, even though sometimes he takes a while to do so because of his hectic schedule. He is really cool. He has done more than what a doctor should do for a patient. He went that extra mile for me so many times, especially when I became very ill and had to be flown back to Toronto by air ambulance. My parents told me that he made all the arrangements and was even at the airport to meet me when we landed. He accompanied me back to Sick Kids and immediately began working on my recovery.

During my last few months at The Hospital for Sick Children, just before I turned eighteen, I had the opportunity to be taken care of by Kathy Johnston, one of the nurses who looked after me as a baby. She told me stories about my first year. I found her to be soft-spoken and caring. She must have been quite gentle with me when I was small. Many other nurses attended to me, but I have to mention her because of my contact with her before I graduated to an adult hospital.

What was different about my situation was the manner in which I was admitted into the hospital over the years. Whenever that happened, I always went straight to the Intensive Care Unit (ICU) because of the critical nature of my illness. It is not a fun place to be because it is only the extremely sick patients who go there. I can remember quite clearly the time when I had to go to the hospital to have my trache removed. With a pillow in my hand, I walked up to the admitting clerk with my parents. My dad told her I had to go to the ICU. She looked at him as if he was out of his mind. I can recall her asking who the patient was. She could not believe that someone could walk off the street and go to the ICU. My dad then told her to call Dr. Edmonds to verify the admission. Similarly, when I was discharged, I left for home straight from the ICU, now known as the Critical Care Unit (CCU).

Although I do not visit The Hospital for Sick Children as often, I still have a special attachment to it and I suppose I always will. I know the doctors and nurses there truly cared. I remain one of their great success stories, one of their miracles and I will never forget all those who cared for me in my home away from home—the renowned Hospital for Sick Children in Toronto.

Chapter 18

College: First Semester

College? Me? A brain-damaged, borderline slow learner? How would I cope? Would I succeed? It was a frightening thought. I did not know anyone in the radio broadcasting programme at Seneca College. We chose Seneca because it was the closest college to our home. My nurse was no longer with me, since nursing care is not funded beyond high school.

I experienced fear, anxiety, stress, and unease. "Were they normal emotions?" I remember asking myself. Too embarrassed to discuss my emotions with anyone, I kept them buried. Even though my parents would try to calm and reassure me, I chose to allow the fright to win the battle.

Seneca@York in Toronto is approximately twenty-five minutes from home, using the highway. The drive on that first morning was long. My stomach was queasy. My legs felt weak. My mom reassured me everything would be fine and that she would help me find the classrooms. That was comforting, in some sense, but it was also embarrassing to have my mom at college with me. However, I could not come up with another solution.

Well, even mom had difficulties finding the room. I quickly realized many normal students were feeling lost. Their expressions said it all. Certainly, that did not help me. I was still experiencing moments of panic.

My first class was English, not one of my favourite subjects. But it was compulsory. I was starting off at a major disadvantage since I did not perform well in the admissions test. As a result, I was accepted into Seneca under certain conditions. I hate tests and never do well on them. I knew I was on probation. My performance that term had to be very good. This was one time I wondered if it was right to be with normal functioning students.

The first class was really a "get to know you" session. Most of my first classes were introductions and outlines of courses. I started to relax.

My mom sat around the college for the first three weeks, sometimes all day. She made sure I developed a good sense of direction and became familiar with the layout of the college. She took me from class to class until I felt comfortable and then she backed off. She met some of my professors and sent them copies of her book. That gave them a better understanding of my problems and based on their feedback, they were amazed I had come so far.

Once I felt confident, Mom began waiting for me in the van in the parking lot. It was very cold, even though it was October but she waited there until I was finished. She did not want to hang around in the school; she wanted me to develop a sense of independence.

Coping with the work was not as tough as I thought. Don't get me wrong—college was no breeze for me! The work was challenging. It meant many, many hours of work. The words of the professors haunted me: "For every hour of work in class, you will have to do two at home." For me? Not two. No way! That would have been too easy.

Memories of my public school principal came back to me. He once told my mom that I should not spend more than forty-five minutes doing work at home. Way back then, I was doing three hours of work a night! It was tedious at times, but I developed really good work habits at an early age. My mom gave me the boost I needed. I say it quite openly and with pride: she was the one who worked with me. She took over my education and tried everything she knew. She always reminded me though, that she could not have taught me if I did not want to learn. Although learning was tough, I wanted to succeed. I wanted to learn. I wanted to be the best I could.

By the way, for my sister and me, watching television was not permitted from Monday to Thursday. We were allowed to watch shows only on Friday evenings, Saturdays and Sundays. Education was always a top priority in our home and distractions like television, radio, or personal stereos were kept to a bare minimum.

With that inner drive, I threw myself into my college courses. My mom continued to be there explaining, simplifying, clarifying, editing and checking to make sure I was coping. How she did it all, I still do not know. She was sick most of the time, suffering from the side effects of the medication she was taking after her cancer treatment. There were days she could not even drive. That first semester was crucial. If I failed, that would have been the end of my college life. Even now it seems so recent in my mind.

God must have given me inspiration. I recall words like *self-centred* and *selfish* coming to mind. Realizing my mom was always there for me, it was my turn to be there for her and prove I could work independently. She and my dad always spoke to me about a positive attitude and the importance of that trait, so I felt it was my turn to give my mom a taste of her own medicine. I kept reminding her that she had to be positive in dealing with her cancer.

My sister, who had just received her driver's license and was attending York University, and my dad transported me to and from college during that period. Some close friends also took time off from their schedule to help us with the transportation. We needed that help. I remember our good friend, Roy Comrie, who one morning ploughed through twenty centimetres of snow to take me to college to write an exam. That was the storm in which the army was summoned to assist with the cleanup! Torontonians will surely long remember the winter of 1999.

Roy came into our lives by chance. After my mom's book was published, there was an article in the *Toronto Star* about it. Roy lived out of town, about two-and-a-half hours east of Toronto. He was painting his home a few months after the book came out. He covered his floor with old newspapers, which he picked up from a local depot. The headline "The Boy Who Wouldn't Die" caught his eye. He phoned around and finally made contact with us through Mrs. Bev Carson at my high school and ordered a copy of my mom's book. After reading it he called us, and since then he has been my parents' adopted little brother and a great source of hope and encouragement to our family.

Even though several things were happening, I managed to keep focused. My broadcasting class met in the auditorium. That was a huge room and I felt lost. The professor was quite good to me. He and the English professor always made sure I understood what was going on without making me feel different or inferior.

The first semester was tough. With my determination to succeed, I worked and worked. My transcript reflected my efforts. Three A's. Unbelievable! With those marks, I was confident I would be accepted into the radio programme. I was admitted and I felt that my efforts were recognized. But the professors did not think I was ready for a full workload.

"Why?" I asked my dad, since my mom was too ill to worry about me.

"They have their reasons, son. They are probably trying to make your life easy."

He remained calm, as usual, and continued. "Attempt the five courses they are suggesting. Remember, it will be a lot of work. No one wants you to be overwhelmed with eight courses."

"Come on, Dad. You know me better than that. I'm no quitter."

Although I knew that I had no choice in the matter, I vented my feelings. "But why do they have to treat me like this? They said that if I was successful with the three courses, they would give me the chance."

"And they have," my father quickly reminded me.

"But on their grounds. And I don't remember it being that way. It was the first term only. Are they going to monitor me for the entire two years?"

"Well, son, that's their prerogative. It may not seem fair, but remember, they will dictate the pace. They have the authority to tell you what you should and should not do. Life is not always fair."

Feeling I was fighting a losing battle, I added, "You know something. It really ticks me off. I'm sure I surprised them with my A's and they still don't have the heart to let me do what I want. I guess I really have no choice but to take their advice."

As tough as the first semester was, it was rewarding. I achieved. I even exceeded my expectations and did it without much help from mom. The fear I experienced the first few days did not matter in the end. I achieved my goal.

Chapter 19

Milestone Celebrations

Where do I begin to write about the milestones of my eighteenth and twenty-first birthdays? I will copy my mom's opening lines she used at my twenty-first birthday celebration: "Let the trumpets sound, let the drums beat and let the music play." Those words told me, in no uncertain terms, my life was worth celebrating. *Trumpets, drums, music*—certainly party words. I do not want to overrate the occasions and the way they were celebrated, but I have to share my great memories.

Both birthday celebrations were formal and they began with a thanksgiving prayer, followed by speeches. Our prayer services are always conducted by one of the most respectable leaders in the Muslim Community, Kaioom Khan. My family admires him for his melodious recitation of the Quran and his practical explanations. He was one of dad's mentors when they both lived in Guyana. My mom, on the other hand, met uncle Kaioom in Canada when I was very ill as a baby and she too, found him very inspirational. He has always been there for us and I have no doubt in my mind that God responded to his sincere and heart-wrenching prayers for me all these years. On my eighteenth and twenty-first birthdays, he spoke emotionally about my struggles and triumphs and more importantly, the power of God.

Each event was held at a banquet hall in Toronto. My mom and my sister chose a jungle theme for my twenty-first birthday, and each table had balloons, which were put together to create a tree-like effect. Each one was stunning. My mom was very ill at the time. She was suffering from Meniere's disease, which she thinks was somehow related to her cancer and was experiencing frequent dizzy spells. I still do not know how things fell into place. My dad, as usual, pulled his weight, but the fine things like the food, desserts and decorating had to be arranged and finalized. Mom somehow got the strength. With the help of two of her friends and Yassy, who flew up from Trinidad just for the weekend to share that special occasion with me, everything came together.

Things went without a hitch. The speeches were deep and sincere. Those on the programme talked about my life and achievements. About four hundred people attended. It was like a wedding reception. My buddy, Dr. Edmonds, spoke at both my eighteenth and twenty-first birthday parties. He said he was not sure when I was a baby how to tell my parents I may not survive. He also went on to say I would have many more challenges to face. He was so right.

The highlight of my twenty-first birthday was world-renowned maestro Tommy Crichlow, playing the steel pan. He mesmerized the audience. Many people felt he should have played more. I can remember Dr. Edmonds smiling and looking closely as the pan was being played. That was a big treat for everyone.

On both occasions there was food and more food. The spreads were huge, with desserts to die for, (date squares, individual cheesecakes, macaroons, fruit platters) especially at my eighteenth birthday. Mom was strong and healthy then, and she makes great low-calorie desserts. She tries recipes and cuts the sugar by more than half and many times reduces the eggs by one or two. With some recipes, she has problems when she cuts back on the eggs, but she works on them until they turn out right.

After the food at my eighteenth birthday party there was socializing. But for my twenty-first it was dancing. That was what I wanted. It was time to party and celebrate with a bang! My friends were there and they had a great time. I opened the dancing with my school friend, Christine. Although it is difficult for me to move freely, I danced and my friends were there supporting and encouraging me.

One of our family friends, Kenty Khan, facilitated both programmes. My dad and Uncle Kenty met at a cricket game in the midsixties, and as far back as I can remember they have been very good friends. Uncle Kenty is very particular about this job. He does a lot of homework before the day and comes prepared with a file full of notes. He makes sure he gets enough background information about everyone on the programme so introductions are appropriate. He adds a lot of humour when there is need for it and becomes very solemn when he has to. He is a lively, well-spoken person to emcee any programme.

At both occasions members from the media—both newspaper and television—were present. At my twenty-first, City Pulse television in Toronto gave me an opportunity that I would always cherish. The reporter asked me to hold the microphone and sign off after he interviewed me. At first I could not believe it, but when he told my parents what he wanted done, I took the microphone and stood there with confidence and said, "This is Azeem Kayum reporting live from Scarborough for City Pulse." That reporter made my day! And thanks to City Pulse for airing it. If they only know broadcasting is one of my passions. For a boy who was diagnosed as one who would never talk, I did it in style at my twenty-first birthday.

Among the guests who attended my eighteenth birthday celebration was the editor of the weekly *Caribbean Camera* newspaper in Toronto, Raynier Maharaj. He chose to write about his impressions in the subsequent issue of this newspaper:

A Miracle Turns 18
By Raynier Maharaj

They called him the Boy Who Would Not Die, and as he took his place in front of a podium recently before some 400 people, it was easy to understand why.

While Azeem Kayum, born here of Trinidad and Guyanese parents, spoke of his own ordeal of living with a rare illness, he spent most of his time at the microphone asking for more tolerance for people with disabilities.

That he could speak at all is a miracle in itself. When he was born 18 years ago, doctors thought he wouldn't live, and that if he did, he would amount to nothing more than a vegetable.

He suffered a spinal defect at birth which, to put it simply, makes his brain go to sleep when he does. This means that his whole body shuts down, and he would die without the use of a respirator to breathe for him.

I've written about young Azeem before, and his life is chronicled in a moving book written by his mother, Trinidad-born Laila, called *For a Breath of Life*.

She and her husband, Scotiabank manager Faizal, originally from Guyana, refused to believe the doctors when they told them their son wouldn't live. Their faith in God and selfless commitment to their child was as much part of the celebration among the invited guests at the recent function in Scarborough, as was the fact that Azeem was turning 18.

Everyone who addressed the gathering agreed that it was the fact that Faizal and Laila chose to keep their son at home, and not institutionalize him, which made the difference in his life.

Not that keeping him home is easy: I know, knowing the family that it required 18 years of total dedication on the part of both parents, as well as that (to a lesser extent only because she is younger) of little sister Lisaan, to accomplish this.

It's not something that many of us would have the courage to do.

Among the audience at the event were a number of people who have worked tirelessly with Azeem since he was born. For one of them, Dr. John Edmonds of the Hospital for Sick Children, Azeem's 18th birthday is bittersweet.

While Dr. Edmonds is thrilled to see the Boy who Would Not Die on the threshold of adulthood—a boy who has been his patient since the age of 6 months—he now has to cut the cord so to speak.

When he turns 18 on December 8, Azeem can no longer be a patient at Sick Kids, which means that Dr. Edmonds as well as his colleagues and nurses who have spent Azeem's entire life with him will have to turn him over to the professionals at Markham Stouffville Hospital.

In his speech, Dr. Edmonds—called by Master of Ceremonies Kenty Khan a "giant among men" for his dedication to his profession—praised Azeem for his courage and thanked him for allowing them to "practice on you." (Because Azeem's case is rare, doctors have been using him to gain more knowledge of his illness, which will in turn benefit other patients in the future.)

He also called on everyone present to work tirelessly to ensure that in this era of health cuts, special care patients like Azeem get the funding they require to help them function as normally as possible.

In turn, Azeem presented Dr. Edmonds, whom he called his "best buddy," with a plaque honoring him for his commitment to his case.

It was indeed a sight, seeing patient and doctor hugging on stage. If one did not know, however, that Azeem still remains a critical case, needing constant care, one would never have guessed it, seeing him looking absolutely dashing in a brand-new suit and walking strongly and bravely on stage.

But though there was speaker after speaker, from doctors to teachers to relatives and friends of the Kayum family, it was Azeem's speech which touched my heart.

In an utterly selfless way, speaking of his own horrific illness as though it was matter-of-fact, he urged people to be more sensitive to the disabled among us.

"Having a disability is not easy," he told the hushed gathering. "No matter what you do, you are treated differently. Disabled people have feelings like everyone else. We all want to have fun, hang out, and be cool. I have it a little harder because I must have adult supervision at school. This is because I can have respiratory problems and end up in trouble. I really do not like having a nurse with me all the time—it just makes me more different."

One could have been forgiven on Sunday for mistaking the ceremony for being a wedding. It had all the trappings of a grand celebration. And while most of us will acknowledge that turning 18 is an achievement, few have ever seen such a glittering ceremony to mark such an event.

But everyone there would heartily agree that there was no more occasion fitting for such a bash.

That Azeem is turning 18 is really a miracle. That he has achieved this milestone is testament not only to his own courage, his ability to laugh in the face of the greatest adversity, but to that of his parents and Lisaan, who are truly remarkable people.

I don't need to ask for them to be blessed. They already are, with a son and brother like Azeem.

Chapter 20

Honours: The Payoff

A summer with eight courses! What had I gotten myself into? My thoughts were running wild. *"Damn. They were probably right— a full workload is definitely turning out to be too much. But I'm not a quitter."*

What made it worse was I had enrolled in a specific course that I absolutely hated. I know *hate* is a strong word, but it's appropriate here. The class was not one of my professional courses but a general education one about poetry. I should not have enrolled in it. I enjoy poetry, but that course was hell for me. My mom had discouraged me from enrolling in it. One of my professors told me I had the option of taking that course or one on economics. My dad told me the economics course would be extremely tough for me, requiring an enormous amount of reading and reasoning. So, as much as I did not want to do it, I enrolled in the poetry course my professor suggested. I needed the course to graduate, because it was compulsory. In addition, it was the only subject that fit into my schedule. I barely managed to survive and escaped with a D.

The following school year was exhausting. I had only a two-week break because I attended school throughout the summer. I needed longer to recover. But I was determined to complete the year. I wanted to graduate on schedule with my friends.

Assignments, written and practical, were piled on. Professors did not care about the workload students had to complete for the other instructors. Each one's aim was to get his or her work done. The students paid the price. I was swamped with work. Some of my peers helped me with the practical aspects of the courses. There were days when I stayed in school until 9 PM, when my parents came to pick me up.

Before graduating, each student was required to complete one hundred hours of fieldwork. Without that, the student would not receive a diploma. After I worked so hard to get good grades, there was the possibility I would not graduate because of this requirement.

Some students were talking about the problems they were having with placement (finding a radio station to complete the required hours). Each one of us had the opportunity to host his or her own radio show at college. That was cool. I looked forward to my weekly hour. The night before my show, I would organize myself and attempt to retrieve some information on some of the artists I would play in my hour. I prepared myself early so I would have enough time at school to look over my notes before going on air. However, those hours of airtime at school were not counted as fieldwork. We all had to go out into the real world. Once again, my parents entered the picture—not that they were ever out of it.

In 1998, an ethnic prime-time morning radio programme was launched in Toronto. It catered to the entertainment and cultural needs of the South Asian and Indo-Caribbean communities. The name of the programme is "Hot Like Pepper Indian Radio," and the broadcast is in English. Within a few months, this show became very popular. Shortly after "Hot Like Pepper" hit the airwaves, my father wrote a letter of congratulations to the producer, Anand Rampersadsingh, and his wife, Ingrid, who is the host of the programme. Over the years my parents kept in contact with both of them. I also delivered two motivational presentations on that station during the Muslim festival of Eid-ul-Fitr.

My mom spoke to Anand about my placement and both he and Ingrid agreed to let me complete my one hundred hours, helping out where necessary. That was a huge relief! Since the staff knew about my disabilities, they would be patient with me. They made me feel very comfortable in their studio and office and provided me with a good understanding of the real broadcasting world. I worked closely with Anand and one of his assistants, Darise Olton. They exposed me to different areas of broadcasting like recruiting sponsors, preparing the log for a three hour show and wording effective commercials. I learned a lot and they treated me with respect and dignity despite my disabilities.

Producing a good programme is not easy. It takes time, dedication, energy and creativity to do so. For me, the hardest part of the job was finding sponsors. Sponsors tried to negotiate better prices, and it was quite frustrating wheeling and dealing with them.

The second year of college ended in April 2002, meaning college life came to an end. Based on the marks posted on the college's Web site, I knew I had passed. Yes, I got a D (50–59%) in the poetry class, but my other marks ranged from A+'s to C+'s. One memorable day I received mail from the college. I suspected it had to do with my transcript. I quickly opened the letter and saw that I was correct. I read the marks and the note that stated I had successfully completed the two-year programme in radio broadcasting. I then read the comments section and I could not believe when I saw the words "Graduated with Honours."

"No, this cannot be. Not me." I tossed the thought out of my head. But, just to make sure, I rushed downstairs and asked my mom. "Do you think they made a mistake?"

She looked at me and smiled. "Why?" She must have suspected it was my marks and in her mind they were high.

"My transcript has 'Honours' written on it. But I'm not sure."

"Let's see. Let's see," she looked excitedly.

"Just what it says. Honours!" she exclaimed. "You did it! You did it! I knew you had it in you! The hard work and long hours brought you success. Yea!"

I saw Mom's happiness. I made her proud. She fussed and carried on. She was more on a high than I was. I never believed I would have passed with honours, especially after that D in poetry. Mom anxiously counted: three A+'s, fourteen A's, nine B+'s, three B's, two C+'s, and one D. I am pretty sure I did the faculty of the Radio Broadcasting department proud. My programme coordinator, Jim Carr, must have felt very accomplished. He followed my progress. My mom kept in touch with him throughout my two years.

Above all, I did myself proud. I achieved something that nobody, except my parents and a few others, thought I could. I quietly gave thanks to God, who guided me, kept me healthy and strong, and carried me during the two years at college. It was not easy, especially dealing with my mom's cancer, the heavy workload and at times, the humiliation of being a special needs student.

That night I spent hours on the Internet e-mailing relatives, especially those in Trinidad. I knew they would be thrilled for me. They had faith in me. They understood how difficult learning was for me. They knew how much I struggled to grasp concepts. They could truly identify with my accomplishment. After all, they monitored my progress since I started school. When my aunts Yassy and Teen visited us during the summer for so many years, they spent hours teaching me, for which I will be forever grateful. To me, that is genuine concern. Can you imagine going on a vacation and spending time teaching a nephew with learning disabilities? Their interest in my development helped keep me going.

I received many e-mails and phone calls once the word got out. Everyone was so proud of me. I could hear the excitement in their voices.

At a private thanksgiving function held at my home to celebrate my graduation from college, two of my cousins, Issa and Nadeem, came from Trinidad for the occasion.

They made me feel very special.

The hard work paid off! I overcame another hurdle. I again went beyond expectations. I graduated from college with honours. I could not have done any better. It was tough, but I did it.

What an accomplishment!

I am very proud of what I did and nobody can take that away from me. The chance I begged for was given to me. I delivered on my promise.

If a child is given a chance, he may prove to be better than what he is given credit for, and I believe I did.

Chapter 21
College Graduation

I had a very tough time getting accepted into college and the challenges I faced during my two years there were extremely difficult. When I had finished the two-year programme, I told my parents in no uncertain terms that enough was enough. "I'm through with studying and I don't want to continue with any more academics," I informed them. At that time, I just wanted to take it easy for the summer before I started looking for a job. I felt my brain was ready to explode and needed a rest. My mom tried to encourage me to spend another two to three years and get my degree, but I was just not interested. In my mind, I had exceeded my own expectations many times over. She backed off and respected my wishes. I still think she would like me to continue my studies, but she does not bring up the subject.

But before considering my future, I had another moment of happiness to enjoy. I was happy not only because of my success, but also because I overcame all the isolation, dealt with the negative comments, and graduated in a programme that entailed speaking. Keep in mind I was not supposed to talk.

Thursday, June 27, 2002, was a great and memorable day for me—college graduation day. It represented the climax of my academic career.

I was allowed to take four guests. My parents, my sister and Dr. Edmonds from The Hospital for Sick Children in Toronto attended the convocation ceremony. Dr. Edmonds was thrilled to be included and cancelled several important appointments to share in my triumph. He was not going to miss it for anything. I would have liked my aunts from Trinidad to be with me, but they would have had to leave their students to do that. If their school year ended in June, they would have been with me.

As we drove to the Living Arts Centre in Toronto, where the convocation ceremony took place, I felt relaxed, satisfied, proud and accomplished. I looked forward to taking the academic stage one last time. We arrived early, and I was quickly gowned and separated from my family. I was one of two people from my class there at the time. Later, the rest of the group came along. Dr. Edmonds arrived about forty-five minutes prior to the scheduled start time of 10 AM. We were asked to line up in alphabetical order and remain that way. As I entered the auditorium with my friends, we took our seats. I looked around, and it reminded me of a setting for an opera. It was a sight to behold.

There were a few hundred students who graduated the same day. We had to wait for at least two hours before the radio broadcasting class was called up. Jim Carr, the programme coordinator, called the names. I was told that when Jim said, "Azeem Kayum," he paused briefly and then added, "Honours."

Was it deliberate? Did he want to stress the "honours" in his own way? I do not know. But I do know that I was ecstatic. I could not have been happier knowing I was being rewarded for all the hard work I did in my school years. The radio broadcasting programme started with twenty-eight students, but only eighteen graduated. Three of those eighteen students graduated with honours and I was one of those. Was I ever proud! My mom, dad, Lisaan and Dr. Edmonds were probably even happier than I was.

My sister told me later that when my name was called, both Dr. Edmonds and Mom jumped out of their seats, cheering, clapping and yelling. Lisaan felt a little embarrassed. I did too, after hearing that. My dad was his usual cool self. I did not even notice what was going on once I was called up. I just chose to focus on and enjoy the moment when I got on the stage to accept my diploma.

Mom and Dr. Edmonds both knew what I went through and they had played critical roles academically and medically to get me to that level. So they were not prepared to hold back their emotions. They just did what came naturally. After the ceremonies were over, my professor, Jim Carr, repeated something he told me a lot during my time at the college: "I wish we had more students like you." He probably was referring to the fact that I did not give up regardless of how difficult the work seemed and no matter how long it took to get something done. I worked very hard to hand in every single assignment on time. I never once asked for an extension.

Here is what my college diploma says:

Chapter 22

My Scholarship Fund

Paul James. The name may seem like a regular one, but to my family it is a special name belonging to a special young man. Paul, a 2003 Seneca graduate in radio broadcasting, was the first recipient of the Azeem Kayum Special Needs Education Scholarship, which was established shortly after I graduated from Seneca College.

The struggles I encountered prior to entering college made my family more aware of the importance of such a fund. Close friends and family helped make this a reality by contributing directly to the scholarship fund. The annual $1,000 scholarship is awarded to a special needs student who demonstrates perseverance, determination and the will to succeed.

Paul was diagnosed at a very young age with a rare congenital vision disorder called achromatopsia. He told us that he endured a lot during his school life. People with achromatopsia are either colour blind or almost colour blind, and they have poor vision. Paul is completely colour blind. Can you imagine living in a world where everything looks black and white and blurred at times?

Despite his condition, Paul is pleasant and friendly. The day I presented him with the award, my mom, Jim Carr (programme coordinator) and Jed DeCory (programme chair) sat and talked for a while. Mom asked Paul how he coped at school. His expression changed as he recalled his earlier years.

"Achieving was not easy. School was always a negative thing for me," he said.

"How so?" my mom questioned. "Look at you today. You have graduated from college."

"I did not have much encouragement from some of the teachers."

"Were they aware of your difficulties?"

"Seeing on the board was hard, even though teachers were aware of my condition."

Paul went on to say that most of the teachers were kind to him, but there were those who didn't take the time to make the necessary adjustments to meet his needs. He felt that others could have helped to make his life a little easier and less stressful. Simple things like placing him at the front of the class would have made a difference. He told us that during public and high schools, he was at the back of the class. That was really sad. I know how he must have felt. I have been there, even though my special needs were different.

"So, Paul, are you working now?" I asked.

"No. I have sent out resumes, but I am always asked whether I can drive. Once I say no, my chances fade."

"Sounds familiar, Paul. So very familiar."

My mom asked Jim why Paul was selected for the award. He said that Paul had shown the determination to succeed. His hard work was evident. It seemed the professors realized that the software used in the programme was not the most appropriate for a student who had problems with vision. There was talk about getting the proper software, but Paul coped with what was available at the time. Paul pointed out that Jim was very helpful.

In selecting the recipients of this award, our family and Jim decided what qualities the student should possess. I felt very happy to give my input, based on my experiences. We agreed that the student must have special needs, be determined, have the drive to succeed and be a hard worker. If there are two or more students who show these qualities, the professors and my family will choose one. But first the two students must write a paragraph or two on why he or she should receive the award.

I sat and listened to Paul. I was hearing my job-hunting experiences being repeated. I shared my stories with Paul. My disabilities are visible. I think they act as a deterrent. During one interview I sensed the discomfort the other person experienced and without asking a question, told me that the position was filled. We have disabilities, but we are also capable. The only way we can prove our capabilities is if we are given the opportunity. Hopefully, Paul and I will one day be given the break we need.

Chapter 23

My Passion

We all have dreams at some stage of our lives. I dream of getting married one day. I dream of being cured. My college education was one step to fulfilling a very special dream. Maybe I should not refer to it as a dream. It has been more like a dream turned into a passion.

When I was around five, I started watching wrestling. Even today, I still watch all the wrestling shows I can. And, no, I do not practise any of the moves, nor do I get fed up watching this sport.

From a young age, I pictured myself welcoming wrestling fans to one of the big events in the city. That desire is still within me today. "Helloooooooooo, Torontooooooooooo!" I imagine myself saying. "Areeeeeeee yooouuuuuuuu rrrrrrreadyyyyyyyyy to ruuummmble?" The crowd roars. The screams echo in my head. I feel the high.

I would like to be a wrestling commentator or do something in the wrestling field. Of course, I could not become a wrestler or a manager. Other wrestlers would likely beat the life out of me with one simple move. But I am sure there is something I can do, even if it is in the office of the WWE (World Wrestling Entertainment).

I have to be realistic. With all my medical problems, it would be very difficult to become a wrestling commentator. The wrestlers and the rest of the crew are on the road most of the year. They move from state to state, country to country. I have my respirator to think about. With my balance, and the weight of the equipment, I could fall many times. I know the company that manufactures respirators has come out with a model similar in size to a laptop computer. However, I've heard it is noisier than the one (LP10) I am currently using. I will wait until they improve the noise factor before thinking of changing my current one. I would also have to check the cost involved. Those machines are not cheap.

Another factor I have to consider is if I become a commentator, I may end up at ringside to do the broadcast. Sometimes those wrestlers are thrown on the table where the commentators sit. If one is thrown when I am there, I would be a goner. I would not be able to move fast enough. That is why, if I were a commentator, I would rather sit near the entrance, as nothing much happens near the broadcast booth in that area.

I will still keep dreaming, though. Perhaps the owner of the WWE may decide to give me the chance. I know dreams do come true. Accommodations could be made for me.

My knowledge of wrestling is great. I do not generally enjoy reading and I suppose it is because of the difficulties I have with comprehension. But give me anything to read on wrestling, and I will devour it. More amazingly, I will understand it. How that happens only God knows, because I have to struggle to understand other material I read.

Even though my dream may never be fulfilled, I will continue to pursue my passion for the sport. Will the WWE give me the chance, the opportunity to experience the high I can only imagine? Only God knows. He has always been on my side, and again, he may work his miracles to give me that opportunity to fulfill my dream.

My experiences with the WWE have been pleasant and enjoyable. I had the opportunity to meet some of the wrestlers personally and attend press conferences. The organization even sent me a special gift for my twenty-first birthday. On another occasion when I appeared on Life Television Network in Toronto, I was surprised when the station set up a live link with one of my favourite WWE wrestlers at the time, Shawn Michaels. Even the president of WWE in Canada, Carl DeMarco, showed up during the interview. That was so cool!

I cannot get wrestling out of my head. Not only do I watch the weekly television shows, I also create my own broadcasts, where I am "Azeem The Dream." The broadcasts going something like this:

> ATD: Welcome, everyone, to Superfights. I'm Azeem The Dream alongside Tommy G. Tonight's show will be like no other. This place is packed to capacity. The crowd cannot wait to get started. Just listen!
>
> TOMMY G: I think you're right, ATD. We should go right to the ring for our opening match as the combatants, Johnny Starr and Richard "The Eagle" Williams, are in the ring just rarin' to go. The bell has just sounded. This match has now officially started.
>
> ATD: The two athletes are locking up. "The Eagle" whips his opponent into the ropes. He's going for a clothesline.
>
> TOMMY G: Johnny Starr is coming off the ropes, ducks the clothesline attempt. He dropkicks "The Eagle." He lands hard on the mat.
>
> ATD: What a move!! He's down … and Starr is going for the early pin, much to the fans delight. 1 … 2 … kickout …

TOMMY G: I don't think you'll pin "The Eagle" this early in the match. But, Starr is coming on strong here, as he is working on the arm. Look at how he is applying the pressure! Look at Starr. He's trying to get to the ropes. But he can't. Look at the pain on his face.

ATD: Yes, he's punishing the arm … trying to rip it out of its socket. Punching the arm … He's stepping on the arm. He pushes "The Eagle" into a corner. Referee asks for a clean break.

TOMMY G: Starr gives it to him, but "The Eagle" has turned it around and is punching Starr in the corner. Those fists are flying.

ATD: He's going for a kick … but Starr moves … Look at him grabbing the legs, pulling him back to the centre of the ring.

TOMMY G: This is brutal—and the fans seem to be enjoying it. Listen to their screams! Starr body slams "The Eagle."

ATD: He's going to the top now … "The Eagle" is already up. This move may cost Starr.

TOMMY G: I don't think so. "The Eagle" is coming closer to Starr, who is perched up on the turnbuckle.

ATD: Starr is inviting him to come. What a move! He's got his legs wrapped around "The Eagle's" head. Oh, my God! "The Eagle" just powered out of the head scissors and super kicked Starr.

TOMMY G: That was great! He's going for the pin. 1 … 2 … kickout. How does he keep kicking out?

ATD: It's the will to win, Tommy. And Starr is acting like he won it.

TOMMY G: He's acting too cocky—saluting the fans. He should keep his eyes on his opponent.

ATD: Wait a minute! I just saw "The Eagle" grab a spray bottle.

TOMMY G: I don't think he'll use it to make himself smell nice!

ATD: I'm thinking the same way, Tommy. Oh, my goodness! He just sprayed some of the cologne into Starr's eye. Starr is going around in circles. He's yelling! He must be seeing stars. Starr is seeing stars!

TOMMY G: He could be blind. He can't see. Looks like he's just fading away.

ATD: No kidding. He's going for the pin. I think he's got him this time. 1 … 2 … 3 … This match is over.

TOMMY G: Richard "The Eagle" Williams has won. Listen to this crowd. They are mad as hell. Can you hear those boos? I think there will definitely be a rematch.

ATD: That's right. Starr was ripped off. We have to take a commercial break.

A break. That is all I need. An opportunity to prove myself. Hopefully, the WWE personnel will one day fulfill that dream!

Chapter 24

My Fears

Who would believe turning eighteen could be so depressing? I felt nervous and anxious.

I did not have those emotions because of the birthday party. Oh no, I was excited about that, but something else was eating me on the inside. Turning eighteen meant a big change, one for which I was not fully prepared. I had to cut ties with "my home away from home," The Hospital for Sick Children. The doctors and nurses knew me there. They were familiar with my medical condition.

Questions were flying around in my head, and I was afraid:

• Can I trust new doctors to keep me alive?

• Will all the new "ologists" be as kind and caring as the ones at my former hospital?

• How will they know if I am really, really sick?

• Will I have to go through a number of tests?

• Will they believe a regular cold can cause me to have really bad breathing problems?

• How will I ever feel secure?

The thoughts were hitting me from all sides. I felt like I was going crazy and I did not know where to turn. My parents were going through their own stresses with this issue. I overheard them talk about new doctors and how different it would be. So I did not want to go to them with my fears.

My parents began doing their homework long before I turned eighteen. They needed recommendations. So whom did they turn to? Dr. Edmonds, of course. The hospital he referred me to was not considered suitable. My parents preferred something closer to home. My mom then began her search. She spoke to two nurses, Pam Laverty and Clytie Scotland, who pampered me while I was a baby at The Hospital for Sick Children. Those nurses left the hospital many years ago.

Mom made some inquiries about a respirologist, Dr. Monique Forse, who is attached to Markham-Stouffville Hospital. She came with high recommendations, but Mom was still not fully convinced. By this time I was becoming restless. The transition was turning out to be worse than I thought. My mom made a few more telephone calls and the feedback she received about Dr. Forse was very promising. Some of the nurses who cared for me at Sick Kids also recommended her. Feeling somewhat satisfied, she called Dr. Edmonds. He had heard about Dr. Forse and made arrangements to have my file transferred to her office.

Mom scheduled an appointment with Dr. Forse, and Dad accompanied us. They wanted to make sure their decision was the right one. Mom did not beat around the bush. She told Dr. Forse about Dr. Edmonds and the concern and personal interest he showed in my care. She added these words, which I will never forget: "We have been very aggressive in trying new forms of ventilation with Azeem. We hope you will not be laid back with his care." Dr. Forse expressed genuine interest and my parents left her office feeling somewhat pleased. They went home and the discussion continued.

"Should we stop, or should we keep on looking?" I heard Mom ask Dad. They spoke at length about Dr. Forse and their meeting. My mom made a few more calls and gathered as much information as possible.

Convinced Dr. Forse was one of the best in the region, they ended their search a few days later. They also asked me how I felt about her. Once I became a teenager, my parents included me in decisions, especially when it came to my health. Since I had a good feeling when I was in her office, I told my parents I felt comfortable.

Dr. Forse was only one of many doctors my parents sought out. My parents turned to her for referrals for an orthopedic surgeon, ophthalmologist, neurologist, allergist and all the other specialists whom I would need to see. Although the transition went well, Dr. Edmonds still remains very special to my family and me.

Fortunately, since I turned eighteen, though traumatic because of the medical changes, my health has improved somewhat. Infections have decreased since Dr. Forse put me on puffers. They keep my airway open, though I am afraid of the long-term use of the powdery stuff I must inhale. I cannot say I enjoy spraying this stuff in my mouth. It is foreign material going into my body. Although Dr. Forse has indicated that the puffers would not harm me, I am still concerned.

So while graduating is usually a happy time for most, that particular graduation was scary, nervous and heartbreaking. I have accepted the fact that the treatment and care I received from the doctors and nurses at The Hospital for Sick Children can never be matched. There was a personal element, a family-like feeling, at that hospital. I have not been to any other hospital as often as I have been to The Hospital for Sick Children. That place was like a security blanket to me.

Another fear I have is suffering before death. I believe that if doctors, nurses and my family did not try their hardest to get me where I am, I would have been dead a long time ago. God has been very good to keep me alive. Although I have lived longer and done more than most people expected of me, I often wonder how much longer I can defy the odds. I just hope when God is ready for me, he takes me quickly.

I worry about the health of my family. While my dad and sister rarely become sick, I know they could possibly become severely ill at any given time and would not be able to care for me. Then what happens? My mom has provided unbelievable care for me. However, as mentioned earlier, in 1999 she was diagnosed with breast cancer and has encountered her share of illness and suffering. She continues to work with me and is supportive at all times. I am also there for her when she needs me. I provide positive advice when she is down, just as she continues to do for me.

Another serious concern I have is whether I will ever become totally independent. Sure, I can do a lot on my own. But I will always need an adult's help with certain things, especially when I become very sick.

That's why my biggest fear is that I could end up in an institution. I hope God protects me from that curse. Living with one curse is enough. I do not want to die trying to cope with another! Despite that, I still worry a lot about Mom and the rest of my family. Who will want to care for me if something happens to them?

The few times my other three family members go out together without me, I remain with a caregiver. I worry about them being involved in a bad crash. What if the three of them die at one time? It may sound far-fetched, but it could happen. What would become of me then? I may end up in Trinidad. That would be cool, because I really and truly feel the love of my relatives there. But then, vacations may not be the same as actually living there. The reality is I would be a burden to others, which I do not want. I hope and pray that God grants my family a long and healthy life and that he takes me before he takes them.

Another worry I have is getting a job. Yes, I completed my two-year course in the radio broadcasting programme at Seneca College. I sent my resumes out to different stations. I have had interviews, but no job offers. The problem is disabled individuals are still looked down upon in society. We are often discriminated against. I am also a member of a visible minority. My skin colour is brown and that does not help.

Some employers perceive the disabled and people with different skin colour as incapable or incompetent. We need to be given the opportunity to prove our worth. If we are given a chance, we can prove to be valuable to any employer. I believe that I have proven myself over and over again. I have not received any job offers, but given the chance at a job, I would learn it and be the best I could be. Then, instead of referring to me as a special needs employee, my employer would refer to me as a special employee, one who works hard, gets the work done and does more than what is expected.

If I do not get a decent-paying job, I will never become financially independent. What will happen to me then? A caring and understanding employer in my field of studies can make a difference in my life and rid me of one of some of my fears.

My independence means a lot to me. I hope someone will realize I'm capable. I have the drive to succeed and I know that if given the chance, I will work very hard and prove to be a good employee. I wonder which employer will remove this fear by reaching out and helping me to use the knowledge and skills I have acquired at school.

Conclusion

Miracles do happen! I am convinced they really do happen. The nurses and doctors refer to me as one of their miracles. Based on what I have endured, I feel that I am a miracle.

I have told the story of my life based on my experiences: brain-damaged, would never walk or talk, could remain a vegetable, slow learner, multiple handicaps and isolation. Weigh those against love, care, interest, help, hard work, determination and perseverance. Those positive elements motivated me to put pen to paper and fingers to keyboard.

When I started writing, I had two major goals: to help my peers deal with their disabilities and to create more awareness about our challenges with the hope that most normal folks will change their opinion about us and not look at us differently. It took me close to four years to complete this book. I did it in between school, applying for jobs and attending interviews. It was not easy, especially for someone who really has to struggle to write. But I was determined and I persevered, as I have done throughout my life.

To the people who face physical and mental challenges on a daily basis, I say keep plugging away. Life will be tough for you, but do not give up. You can achieve. If I can achieve, so can you. Set high goals and work toward them. Remain positive and be close to people who believe in you. Have faith in those who care, in those who encourage you, in yourself and in your God.

Those who sneer, snub and stare have a great deal of maturing to do. Maybe they do not know how to cope with or understand those who are different. Everyone should attempt to use his strengths and strive to reach his potential. I think I am blessed—blessed with caring parents, a sister, grandparents, aunts and uncles, a great set of family friends and my personal friends! I am fortunate. I wrote of their support throughout my book because I believe it has helped me and will continue to help me to move ahead.

My parents are happy that I have another accomplishment under my belt—writing this book. Even though they knew that I had several bad experiences, they were taken aback to learn how much hurt, pain and humiliation I have felt. Those feelings were buried inside me for many years.

Although I am not as capable as the normal person, I thank God for blessing me in a very special way. He gave me the gift to know when people are not genuine. Oh yes, I can tell! When people have to make an effort to approach me, I know they do not want to have a conversation with me. Sometimes their tone of voice sends a negative message to me. Then, I have people who truly care. Those people are important to me. They show true love and compassion. They keep in touch regularly to find out how I am doing.

I think everyone, including those who are normal, should read this story. Normal people may learn how to treat those who are disabled. They will be more aware of our feelings, and *we do have feelings*.

I have been critical in some of my comments. I have endured pain from the able-bodied people. By saying what I did, I am reaching out, trying to communicate with those normal people, trying to tell them that although I do not appear normal in their eyes, I have feelings just like them. And yes, I am trying to help these people understand those who are challenged. If after reading about my experiences, some readers change their attitude toward the disabled, I will have accomplished yet another victory.

My life will continue to be a struggle. However, I will always try to surround myself with positive people. I will keep focused and dream my dreams.

I am different
Will be for a long time
Perhaps forever.
In my mind,
I am a perfect me
Despite my disabilities.
I would like to remove
The tracheostomy tube.
That may be distant
But a wish all the same.
Even if I am not like everyone else
I would like to be
The best I can
And will always strive
To improve myself
Each and every day.

In closing, I will say again it is the people who showed their love, who spent time with me, who were not ashamed of me and who encouraged me, it is those people who have helped me. They are the ones who nudged me to change the things others see as different into something to be proud of. They are the ones who showed me I could hold my head up high and walk proudly, even though I will continue to have limitations and shortcomings. They are my mentors, my guides. They are the ones who saw only my strengths and taught me how to see through and overcome barriers. They encouraged me to savour my victories and never ever quit. What a lesson to learn!

Thanks to all who showed me the road to success.

Addendum

After the publication of the first edition of this book in 2004, my life took an unbelievable turn. Doors were opened by yet another angel—a school superintendent, Vicki Bismilla, who looked beyond my disabilities. She read my book and felt that my story would weave in well with the board's character education initiative. She informed the principals in her area about the character traits I developed and their response enabled me to launch a career in motivational speaking.

I use my life story to encourage students to be the best they can. I tell them how I developed the "I Can" attitude and encourage them to truly believe in their abilities. My presentations include lessons on perseverance, respect, inclusiveness, courage, fairness, optimism, caring, responsibility, empathy and compassion. I touch on the importance of faith, initiative, confidence and self-esteem.

I have also done a few corporate presentations, where I stress the importance of looking beyond disabilities and focus instead on the abilities of potential employees.

In June 2006, I was the tribute speaker at Seneca College's convocation, where I addressed the graduates of several programmes.

The following year I was the keynote speaker at Centennial College's convocation, where I addressed the graduates of the School of Community and Health Studies.

In March 2007, I received the York Region Character Advocate Award at the Community Council's inaugural event. As a result of this award, I was selected as an associate member of the Character Community Council of York Region.

I am now enrolled in a distance education program working towards my degree in communications. It may take me several years to complete because my parents are against me attempting more than one course at a time. I am convinced that one day I will graduate with my bachelor of professional arts.

Bibliography

Baksh Kayum, Laila M. *For a Breath of Life*. Canada. A.I.F. Publishing, 1995.

Goldhar, Kathleen. "Teen who's battled handicap wins award for achievement," *Toronto Star,* July 17, 2006, A6.

Harvey, Robin. "The boy who wouldn't die," _Toronto Star,_ March 1, 1996, D4.

Maharaj, Raynier. "A miracle turns 18," *Caribbean Camera*, Dec. 4, 1997, 4.

Azeem's inspiring life story, his resilience and relentless determination have impressed many audiences. If you would like him to speak at your school, meeting, conference, or convocation, please contact him at:

(905) 294-4800

azeem@sympatico.ca

www.azeemkayum.com

Wrestling with the Goddess details the candid, personal journey of one man's struggle with a debilitating and chronic illness, the insurmountable challenges he faces and his eventual realization that first and foremost, he must believe in himself.

Most human beings strive for greatness in their lives. Azeem Kayum's only wish is to be normal. After suffering a spinal cord injury at birth that results in severe neurological damage, he must begin to deal with a disability that impairs his verbal and comprehension skills, and also leaves him with the inability to reason and process information quickly.

Confronted with constant social, academic and physical challenges, Azeem must frequently remind himself that he is not a quitter and soon learns that his pure zest for life will help him overcome countless obstacles. Without realizing it, he begins to achieve greatness through hard work, courage and a dogged determination to not only survive, but also thrive, despite all odds. Azeem's story is an eye opener for those who consider themselves normal and undoubtedly a wonderful inspiration to others with disabilities.

Azeem's message is simple. Reach for the stars. They may seem far. Persevere and you will get there because anything is possible with the right attitude.

Printed in the United States
by Baker & Taylor Publisher Services